5—

A. South

Peninsula Pilgrimage

PENINSULA PILGRIMAGE

By Elizabeth Valentine Huntley

The Pyne Press
Princeton

Library of Congress Catalog Card Number 74-78572

Printed in the United States of America

This Pyne Press edition is a
republication, unabridged and unaltered, of
original material published by The
Press of Whittet & Shepperson,
Richmond, Va., 1941.

This book is respectfully dedicated
to the Men and the Women
who have saved old places from the ravage of time
and have restored them to their original
charm and beauty

Introduction

A DELIGHTSOME ADVENTURE is offered motorists in the unusual tour Mrs. Huntley describes in this book. Most of those who have visited the Peninsula of Virginia in the past have gone from Richmond to Williamsburg, have enjoyed its restored splendors and, after side trips to Yorktown and to Jamestown, have returned to Richmond by the same main highways. Mrs. Huntley suggests and charmingly illustrates a more interesting route. Past the famous estates and some less known old homes in Henrico and Charles City, she carries the visitor by way of the Old Indian Trail. This road is one of the loveliest in Eastern Virginia. It crosses past broad-acred plantations and winds through woods concerning the beauties of which there is only one question—whether they are more alluring in the myriad greens of spring or in the throne colors of autumn. After the traveler has enjoyed this road, has seen the great mansions on the North bank of the James, and has stood under the eaves of Charles City Courthouse, Mrs. Huntley conducts him down to the Chickahominy River, across the new bridge at Barret's Ford and on to Williamsburg. Her notes on the second Colonial Capitol do not duplicate what is said in the exhibition buildings by the hostesses of the Williamsburg Restoration. Mrs. Huntley waits outside the Palace, the Capitol and the Raleigh Tavern, so to speak, while the guest is being conducted through them, and then she takes him on the rounds of all the old homes of the town. From Williamsburg the tour goes on to Carter's Grove and to Yorktown and back, up the glorious York, through Williamsburg by the shortest route and along the smooth road to sacred Jamestown, "cradle of the republic."

Instead of returning directly from Jamestown to Richmond, Mrs. Huntley takes her guests across the ferry and lands at Scotland Neck. Until the moment of leaving Jamestown, the journey is over familiar ground, where the excellence of Mrs. Huntley's guidance is chiefly in the ease of her itinerary and the novel features of her narrative. From Scotland Neck to Richmond, she conducts the tourist over roads that are little traveled, to neglected churches seldom visited, and to some homes of great age that remain much as they were a hundred years ago. Claremont and the Brandon estates she of course includes, but these she approaches from the direction opposite that of most pilgrimages. Usually these interesting old mansions are reached by traversing one of the James River Bridges at Richmond and by motoring through heavy traffic until Hopewell or Petersburg lie behind.

For this treatment of the "South Side of the James" as essentially one with the Peninsula, Mrs. Huntley has the amplest historical justification. Prior to the construction of the railroad from Norfolk to Petersburg, the way to the homes in Surry and in Prince George was the same as that to Henrico and Charles City, namely up James River. As Mrs. Huntley is at pains to point out, the confines of Jamestown at one time included an area on the right bank of the river, precisely as the District of Columbia until 1847 incorporated the City of Alexandria and the county of the same name, now Arlington. Still again, social interests, old family names and in some instances even the ownership of land were identical on both sides of the lower James. The only reason that the South Side did not boast as many great homes as the left bank was that, in early colonial days, the settlers chose the sites on the estuaries, along the creeks or immediately adjacent to the river itself. Water transportation was, of course, the great desideratum. On the whole, it was better on the North Side than on the South. Along the Rappahannock, the development was somewhat different because the flats facing the river were infested with mosquitoes. The great planters established themselves on higher ground which sometimes was a mile or more inland.

No less happy than the scope of her tour has been Mrs. Huntley's choice of a title—"Peninsula Pilgrimage." A pilgrimage it verily is! Whether the district be viewed in the chronology of settlement or simply in the order that the stirring plantations are visited, one is conscious of a certain brooding presence of great spirits. Is it by the seawall at Jamestown that one sits and pictures the three little ships tacking their course up the river that May day in 1607? John Smith was aboard, Smith who embodied as stoutly as Frobisher or Raleigh the adventurous manhood that found England an island and made her an empire. Does

8

one go alone into the quiet of the little church on the island and, disregarding modern tablets and exalted epitaphs, gaze at the foundations of the earlier edifice? One thinks of them as the stones of self-government in the Western world. Holy ground it is, ground where stood those who, in 1619, ere the *Mayflower* left England, began a new democracy among men. At Williamsburg, the feeling is the same. If one waits until the rush of the day is over and silence has fallen on the Capitol enclosure, one almost may hear the defiant voice of Patrick Henry as he cries, "If this be treason, make the most of it!" Surely the tall figure of George Washington will emerge in a moment from the doorway, perhaps to pass an excited, tawny-haired young student named Thomas Jefferson. If lights are bright in the Raleigh Tavern, the tinkle of lifted glasses proclaims a toast to the new declaration of independence, or celebrates the birth of the Phi Beta Kappa Society. The newest book in the shop-window is Richard Bland's "Inquiry into the Rights of British Colonists." That soldier, forever scribbling love-knots and hearts and monograms in his note-book, while George Wythe expounds the law in the study of his home is Colonel John Marshall. If these be not men to whose fanes a pilgrimage is an inspiration, then the heart of America is past stirring, and history no longer teaches men to hope.

"Peninsula Pilgrimage"—and on a narrow peninsula at that. From an airplane, the James and the York seem branches of the same stream. In a motor car, one may pass in half an hour from one to the other. That small area east of the Chickahominy and bounded by the other rivers, witnessed the first sure establishment of an English home in America, the planting that began our agriculture, the forges that forecast our industries, the earliest law-making body in the colonies, the initial proposal for a college to serve the sons of settlers, the nascent stirrings of the spirit of independence, the amplest social life of a graceful era, and, after a century, the opening conflict of the war that shattered and then rewelded America. What a drama, but how human the actors! There was no *deus ex machina* from overseas to resolve the tragedy of the colonists. Neither was there any unique virtue in their order of living that produced great men. They had in tobacco a staple that brought merchantmen from the Thames to the James. Once that staple became profitable, there was in Virginia none of the isolation of a colony founded and forgotten. On the contrary, sons went back to England for their schooling; cousins crossed the Atlantic to visit the frontier

9

and returned to tell tall tales; women hailed with zest the arrival of every familiar ship, because it brought new bonnets. Inland the plantations spread, as old lands no longer supplied the demand for tobacco; but homeward the Virginian colonials looked for a century and more. In spirit, they were prosperous English squires or lesser nobility, who were proud of their stock and able to enjoy some of the luxuries of their kinsmen's craft. If the great families of the eighteenth century came from an area relatively small, the reason was simple: those diligent managers who had numerous slaves on large farms close to the navigable rivers could send enough tobacco overseas to produce an income sufficient to assure them a standard of living similar in all essentials to that of rural England.

No, there is no magic, no mystery, no miracle, in the soil of the Peninsula of Virginia. It was an economical area of production for a foreign market; it was the natural seat of government and the logical site for the first college; but by 1765 it had begun to lose its supremacy. At least two of the great political revolutionaries, Henry and Jefferson, and many of the military commanders were not associated directly with the economic order of the Peninsula or of the nearby river valleys. That which made Tidewater society dynamic in leadership was a well-nigh universal sense of responsibility. This, in a measure, had its origin in the limitation of the franchise to land-owners who chose as Burgesses those who had the heaviest stake in the existing order. In part, also, responsibility was paternalistic, and in part it was religious. The parish vestry, which long had administrative duties, consisted usually of the wealthiest planters who were not always the most pious men of the county. However compounded, this responsibility was seriously regarded and seriously discharged. This does not mean that they were no wastrels, no drunkards. Bankruptcy was not infrequent, gambling was prevalent; men could drink themselves to death in Williamsburg as readily as in London. Neither did the sense of responsibility of the great planters postulate their political unity. The large number of Tories among them at the time of the Revolution is sufficient evidence to the contrary. What does stand out, clearly and with fine dignity, is that most of those who had intelligence, knowledge and experience placed it at the command of their countrymen less favored. Some travelers who go with Mrs. Huntley on her Peninsula Pilgrimage may return from it, perhaps, with the conviction that the spirit which made Virginia great may, if reawakened, make America greater.

DOUGLAS SOUTHALL FREEMAN

S P O N S O R S

O F AN IMPORTANCE to the publication of this book equal to that of the author has been the encouragement and support offered by these book lovers whose interest in the charm of the older places in Virginia have made this book a reality:

Contents

WILLIAMSBURG *(Continued)*

RICHMOND TO WILLIAMSBURG
BY WAY OF
OLD INDIAN TRAIL

Route 5

	Highway Mileage	Mileage off Highway

RICHMOND
(See Map)

Capitol Square, Richmond, Virginia	.0	
Go south to Main Street, east on Main Street to Lester Street, on Lester to Williamsburg Avenue, turn right on Old Indian Trail, Route 5.		
Tree Hill (Private Residence)	4.3	
Wilton Historical Marker for original site	.7	
Varina, by way of Richmond National Battlefield Park sign (Private Residence)	2.4	10.0
Curles Neck (Private Residence)	4.9	5.0
Turkey Island Monument	.9	
Malvern Hill site	.5	
Dogham (Private Residence)	3.3	1.3
Riverview Farm (Private Residence)	.4	2.6
Shirley (Private Residence, Admission to Garden 50¢) . . .	.5	3.8
Turn right off highway to Berkeley and Westover (Private Residences)	3.2	6.4
Berkeley (Residence and Grounds, Admission 75¢)		
Westover (Admission to Garden 50¢)		
Westover Church	1.7	.6
River Edge (Private Residence)	3.4	.7
Greenway (Private Residence)	1.3	
Charles City Court House	.5	
Bush Hill (Private Residence)	.5	
Turn right off highway to The Weyanokes (Private Residences)	1.0	9.4
Sherwood Forest (Private Residence)	2.0	
Bridge	9.8	
Williamsburg	10.3	

WILLIAMSBURG
(See Map)

WILLIAMSBURG TO YORKTOWN
BY WAY OF
POCAHONTAS TRAIL

Route 60

	Highway Mileage	Mileage off Highway
Williamsburg—William and Mary College West on Duke of Gloucester Street to Pocahontas Trail, Route 60	.0	
Carter's Grove (Private Residence)	6.8	1.3
Martin's Hundred Historical Marker	1.4	
Turn left on Route 174	.7	
To Route 170	1.1	
Turn right to Yorktown	4.1	
Battlefield Tour		12.5

YORKTOWN
(See Map)

YORKTOWN TO WILLIAMSBURG
BY WAY OF
COLONIAL NATIONAL PARKWAY
THROUGH WILLIAMSBURG TO ENTRANCE OF
WILLIAM AND MARY COLLEGE   28.3

WILLIAMSBURG TO JAMESTOWN
BY WAY OF
ROLFE HIGHWAY

Route 31   6.4

JAMESTOWN
(See Map)

20

JAMESTOWN TO RICHMOND
BY WAY OF
COLONIAL TRAIL

Route 10

	Highway Mileage	Mileage off Highway
Jamestown Ferry Daily schedule: on the hour, 7 a.m. to 9 p.m. Sundays and holidays: 7 a.m. to 11 p.m.		
Scotland	.0	
Smith's Fort Plantation on Rolfe Highway Route 31 (A. P. V. A. Admission 25¢)	2.4	.5
Surry County Court House	1.9	
Turn left on Colonial Trail, Route 10 to Chippokes (Private Residence)	4.5	5.0
Lower Surry Church, Lawnes Creek Parish	1.9	
Bacon's Castle, turn left at Bacon's Castle marker (Private Residence)	.4	1.3
Center of Town of Smithfield	11.3	
Through Smithfield, to St. Luke's Church entrance gate . .	4.4	.2
Leaving St. Luke's Church, returning to Surry County Court House	22.8	
Glebe House (Private Residence)	4.7	
Turn right at Spring Grove on Patrick Henry Highway, Route 40		4.2
Eastover sign on Patrick Henry Highway, Route 40		.3
Eastover gates (Private Residence)		5.2
Leaving Eastover gates, return to Eastover and Claremont Ferry signs, make sharp right turn		6.0
Claremont Manor gates (Private Residence)		5.1
Leaving Claremont Manor gates, turn right at Y fork, 1.1 miles to Cabin Point on Colonial Trail, Route 10	4.5	
Cabin Point, turn right at Burrowsville	3.5	
Brandon (Private Residence)		5.5
Upper Brandon (Private Residence) turn right at Brandon stables		3.3
Turn right to Colonial Trail, Route 10		1.8
To Brandon Church, bear to right	5.0	
Colonial Trail, Route 10, turn right by Hopewell Railroad tracks	13.5	
Go from Hopewell Street to Broad; turn right, continue to Cedar Lane, turn left, continue to Appomattox Manor (Private Residence)	1.6	
Leaving Appomattox Manor, enter business district to Randolph Street, turn right on Colonial Trail, Route 10, to U. S. Route 1	9.3	
Turn right to Hull Street over downtown route, cross Mayo Bridge, turn left on Main Street to Ninth Street, turn right to Capitol Square, Richmond, Virginia	13.6	

HENRICO COUNTY

HENRICO COUNTY, VIRGINIA

BECAUSE the first permanent settlers of the oldest Anglo-Saxon Colony in North America were Englishmen of the Elizabethan era, they brought with them the law, the outlook, and the customs of the old country. Virginia, christened for the "Virgin Queen" was, to these settlers, an outpost of England, where they proposed to preserve the "well-remembered names" of the homeland. Almost every landscape that recalled a familiar scene was styled after the English original. New estates, created in the wilderness, were given old titles. In those instances where no associations were found, the names used by the Indians were adopted. Some of these were euphonious and rhythmic. Some were harshly unpronounceable. The settlers were patriots also, and they memorialized the royal family in stream and shire. Thus it came about that the eight geographical units into which the colony first was divided in 1634 did honor to Stuarts and, in contrast, saved for posterity two Indian names. These shires were Henrico, James City, Charles City, Elizabeth City, Warwick River, Warrosquyoak subsequently Isle of Wight, Charles River later York County and Accawmack (Accomac). Our tour of the Valley of James River begins the first of these shires, Henrico, itself named after Henrico Town, so designated in 1611, as a tribute of allegiance to Henry, Prince of Wales.

RICHMOND

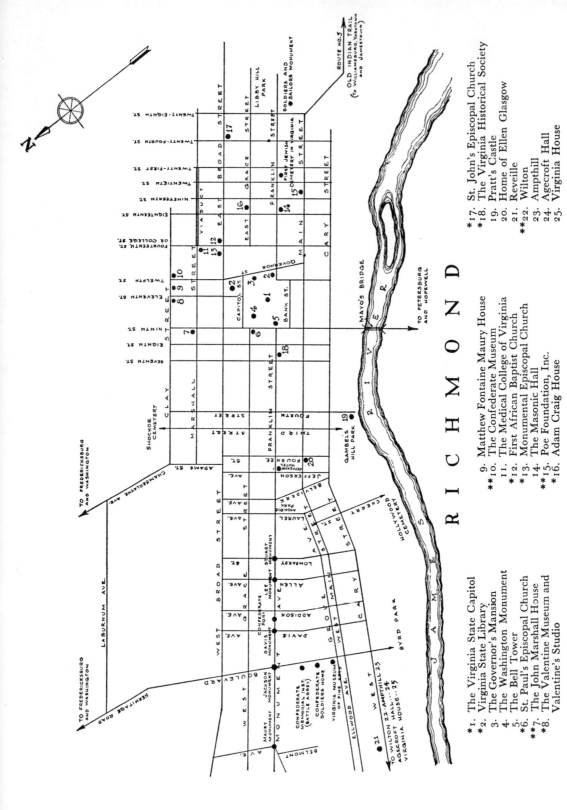

RICHMOND

*1. The Virginia State Capitol
*2. Virginia State Library
3. The Governor's Mansion
4. The Washington Monument
*5. The Bell Tower
*6. St. Paul's Episcopal Church
**7. The John Marshall House
*8. The Valentine Museum and Valentine's Studio
9. Matthew Fontaine Maury House
**10. The Confederate Museum
11. The Medical College of Virginia
*12. First African Baptist Church
*13. Monumental Episcopal Church
14. The Masonic Hall
**15. Poe Foundation, Inc.
*16. Adam Craig House
*17. St. John's Episcopal Church
**18. The Virginia Historical Society
19. Pratt's Castle
20. Home of Ellen Glasgow
21. Reveille
**22. Wilton
23. Ampthill
24. Agecroft Hall
25. Virginia House

* Open to the Public.   ** Open to the Public—Admission charged.

RICHMOND, VIRGINIA

ALMOST IMMEDIATELY after landing at Jamestown, Captain Christopher Newport and John Smith, with a small company, explored the James River to the Falls and here visited the native Indian Chief, "Little" Powhatan. This was probably the first appearance of the white man in these parts and was the first step toward the founding of Richmond.

After 1620, or thereabouts, the colonists maintained, with some intermissions, a fort at the falls. Various Indian fights, the details of which have been lost, occurred in the vicinity of Richmond. Little authentic history prior to 1733 survives. In that year Colonel William Byrd of Westover, the second of that name, visited the site, and under date of September 19, made this entry in his journal: "When we got home we laid the foundation of two large cities, one at Shacco's, to be called Richmond, and the other at the falls of the Appomattox River, to be named Petersburg. These, Major Mayo offered to lay out into lots without fee or reward. The truth of it is, these two places being the uppermost landing of James and Appomattox rivers, are naturally intended for marts, where the traffic of the outer inhabitants must center. Thus we did not build castles only, but also cities, in the air."

Four years later, when Richmond was laid off into a town, the original lots were offered for sale by lottery. In 1742, the growing settlement was incorporated formally as a town, and, after another twenty years, was granted a charter as a city.

During the early years of the revolution, Williamsburg, the second colonial capital, was so much exposed to attack by the British that the General Assembly decided to remove the seat of government inland. By a close vote, in 1779, Richmond was chosen the third Capital of the Old Dominion. After years of slow growth and a period of rapid development in the eighteen thirties, Richmond was chosen in May, 1861 the Capital of the Confederate States of America. The reason, curiously enough, was the reverse of that which had led to its selection in 1779: it was made the Capital of the new Southern government because it was near the exposed frontier of the Confederacy and was close to the fields of anticipated battle.

Today, Richmond, the Capital of Virginia, is a thriving industrial city many times its original size and considered very beautiful, especially in the early spring. Beginning at the Capitol, in Capitol Square, we shall visit only the historical places of interest still standing. These points of interest are scattered in various sections of the city namely, Old Richmond, Court End, Tobacco District and present day residential. They are identified by numbers on the map of the city.

THE VIRGINIA STATE CAPITOL

Capitol Square

Ninth Street facing West Grace Street · No. 1 on Richmond map

AS PREVIOUSLY MENTIONED, after many debates and a close vote, in 1779, the General Assembly of Virginia moved the capital from Williamsburg to Richmond. The following May, the legislators met in a temporary Capitol on the northwest corner of Cary and Fourteenth Street; then known as "the foot of Council Hill on Pearl" or "the street leading to Mayo's Bridge, next door to the Rising Sun Tavern and near the Main Road." It was at this session that an act was passed "for creating the Publick Square, to enlarge the town of Richmond and for other purposes." The same General Assembly also passed the resolution which waived Virginia's claims to the Northwest territory.

The permanent site chosen for the new Capitol was Shockoe Hill, part of which, on August 17, 1784, was bought from Thomas Newton, Junior and John Woodson. One year to the day, the cornerstone for the Capitol was laid. The designs for the edifice were made in Paris, by Jefferson and Clérisseau, after the Maison-Carrée, a Roman Temple at Nimes, France. The Assembly met in the new building for the first time October 28, 1788. At the turn of the twentieth century the Capitol was greatly enlarged by the construction of broad granite steps and by the addition of the two wings, the Western for the Senate and the Eastern for the House of Delegates. While these chambers have been the scene of many notable enactments, the central building, "the old Capitol," naturally holds most interests for the visitor because of the great dramas of American history staged on the stout old foundations. At the close of the eighteenth century, John Marshall, later to become Chief Justice of the United States, delivered an oration on George Washington. Several years later, as Chief Justice, he presided in the old House of Delegates at the treason trial of Aaron Burr. In 1824 Marshall here conducted a meeting for the organization of the Colonization Society, designed to provide homes in Africa for Negroes then in bondage.

During the War between the States, with Richmond as the Capital of the Confederacy, the ebb and flow of the Southern cause was registered. Robert Edward Lee, late Colonel of the first Regiment of Cavalry U. S. A. received in the capitol his commission as "Commander of the Military and Naval forces of Virginia." On the spot where Lee was welcomed by the Virginia convention now stands Rudulph Evans' graceful and inspiring statue of this great Southern hero. In February, 1862, the first permanent Confederate Congress assembled in the legislative chambers. Four days later, on an improvised platform in front of the Washington Monument, in the Capitol Square, President Davis and Vice-President Stephens took their oath of office under Judge J. D. Halyburton, of the Confederate Circuit Court. Very different was the scene in May, 1863, when weeping thousands passed through the rotunda and into the House of Delegates to gaze for the last time on the ascetic face of "Stonewall" Jackson as he lay in state. That was the beginning of the end. Early on the morning of Monday April 3, 1865, amid shouts and screams of panic stricken women and children and sounds of galloping hoofs on cobble stone streets, the United States Flag was run up on the Capitol, where the Military Governor, Brigadier-General Shepley, established his temporary headquarters.

In the winter of 1870, nearby streets rang with the cheerful voices of countless negro news boys as they shouted Virginia's readmittance into the Union. A joyful crowd gathered in the Capitol Square. By order of General Canby a salute of one hundred guns was fired in celebration of the great occasion.

The latter part of April the Virginia Court of Appeals met to decide the heated question as to who was the Mayor of the City of Richmond, Henry K. Ellyson, appointed under the reorganized State Government, or George Chahoon, the military appointee under General Canby. The old hall of the House of Delegates was packed to its capacity. Suddenly there was a loud explosion, a terrific crash, followed by shrieks and groans from the many victims crushed beneath the flying timbers. The gallery had given away. This was indeed "the Capitol Diaster." The decision later rendered was in favor of Mayor Ellyson.

One should not fail to visit the old hall of the House of Delegates, on the north side of the Rotunda, which is reached by taking the elevator on the ground floor. The last session of the House of Delegates ended here in March 15, 1904 and since its restoration in 1929, although used for various meetings, the old hall has become a memorial to Virginians who reached distinction before the close of the War Between the States. Around its walls, in niches and on pedestals are statues and busts of these famous Virginians. Lining the walls in the halls and along the stairways leading to the gallery of the Rotunda are portraits of Queen Elizabeth, Captain John Smith, and all of the Governors of Virginia.

WASHINGTON STATUE

The Rotunda

The Capitol, Capitol Square

THE CHIEF ADORNMENT and the greatest treasure of the Capitol is the marble statue of George Washington, the only one, moulded from life, now in existence. This exquisite work, to which time has given an ivory cast, was authorized by resolution of the General Assembly June 22, 1784. At the instance of Thomas Jefferson Jean Antione Houdon, the famous French sculptor received the commission. The following fall Houdon took measurements and casts of Washington, at Mount Vernon. After his return to Paris, he completed the statue in 1788. Although the pedestal is somewhat too high for the best view of the statue, those who will mount the moveable platform in the rotunda (no charge, move the platform at will) can study what Lafayette termed "A fac-simile of Washington's Person."

The inscription on the pedestal, attributed to James Madison, is as follows:

"George Washington. The General Assembly of the Commonwealth of Virginia have caused this statue to be erected, as a monument of affection and gratitude to George Washington; who uniting to the endowments of the hero the virtues of the patriot, and exerting both in establishing the liberties of his country, has rendered his name dear to his fellow-citizens, and given the world an immortal example of true glory. Done in the year of Christ, one thousand seven hundred and eighty-eight, and in the year of the Commonwealth the twelfth."

When the General Assembly passed the resolutions for the Statue of Washington it also passed one "ordering that a bust of Lafayette, ordered in 1781 be put in the same place with the statue of Washington." The Lafayette bust, also by the hand of the famous Houdon, with busts of the seven Virginia born Presidents of the United States are in the Rotunda, in the niches surrounding Houdon's Washington. The Virginia Presidents are: Thomas Jefferson, by Attilio Piccirilli, from the original by Houdon; James Madison, by F. William Sievers; James Monroe, by Attilio Piccirilli; William Henry Harrison, by Charles Beach; John Tyler, by Charles Keck; Zachary Taylor, by F. William Sievers, and Woodrow Wilson, by Harriet W. Frishmuth.

VIRGINIA STATE LIBRARY
AND SUPREME COURT OF APPEALS

Capitol, Broad, Governor and Eleventh Streets

No. 2 on Richmond map

AT THE FOOT of the steep granite steps near the east end of the Square, is the "old" State Library Building which was completed in July, 1895. Until recently it housed approximately two hundred and ninety thousand books, together with many valuable maps, old newspapers, periodicals, historical documents and over a million manuscripts. The extension division of the State Library, with over sixteen thousand volumes, had headquarters adjoining those of the archives department. The model of the Maison-Carrée, at Nimes, France, which Thomas Jefferson brought over from France for the design of the original Capitol, was in the reference library on the third floor where, also were a number of very interesting paintings and portraits. On the ground floor of the "old" Library there still is a room devoted to an exhibition of Virginia minerals, timber and specimens of natural history. This is under the supervision of the State Conservation Department. The Library building is open daily from half past eight in the morning until half past four in the afternoon, except on Saturdays when it is closed at noon.

One could spend hours strolling up and down the uneven old brick pathways which lead to the various statues immortalizing historically prominent persons, and wandering over Capitol or Council Chamber Hill. Richmond like Rome is built on seven hills, the names of which vary through the long and changing years but the list originally suggested by the City Council is: Union Hill, Church Hill, Gamble's Hill, Council Chamber Hill, French Garden Hill, Shockoe Hill and Navy Hill.

Several of these locations have been preserved for public parks but it is certain not one is as lovely and inviting as Capitol Hill. Here one may sit beneath age old trees listening to the musical sounds of the tinkling fountain and watch the busy little squirrels capering from limb to limb. If one is historically minded he may dream of Richmond in by gone days, while viewing from any angle, modern Richmond amid the hurry and noise of twentieth century existence.

Turning one steps towards the new library, pass the Governor's Mansion and leave the square by way of one of the large entrances, which at intervals break through the tall iron fence built in 1819. Tradition says this enclosure was erected by a fastidious aristocrat who resented the pasturing of marketable live stock so near the Governor's Mansion.

The new State Library Building of Indiana limestone and polished pink Salisbury granite is modelled along modern lines adapted from the classic architecture. The entrance to this magnificent edifice is on the south or Capitol Street side. Upon entering, one ascends a flight of pink Tennessee marble steps across the top of which is a bronze grilled gateway. The main hall is panelled in oak and is finished in antique gray with a black Belgian marble base. The floor is of two toned gray marble laid in squares and outlined in bronze. The lighting arrangement is as beautiful as it is interesting. The ceilings throughout are of acoustic tile.

To the left and right of this great hall one looks through huge bronze and plateglass entrances into the reading rooms. These spacious quarters are panelled to the sills of the many and well regulated double windows which reach to the high ceilings. The walls are painted a soft gray-green while the floors are of a darker gray.

The private offices of the librarian and his assistants together with the cataloguing department and individual work rooms, cover the second floor. In the first basement are the storage and stock rooms. The second basement is used for the photostat room, shipping station and the rare book sanctuary.

Approaching the building from Broad Street one enters a large foyer of domestic Travertine marble. Taking the elevator to the third floor one steps into a square hall, beautifully panelled in walnut, which leads to the court room of the Supreme Court of Appeals. To the left as one enters the hall is located a modern and well arranged law library leading from which is a long corridor extending southwardly along Governor Street, the entire length of Capitol Street and thence northwardly along Eleventh Street, to the court of appeals.

Along this corridor are situated the private offices, chambers and conference rooms of the Justices. Here also are various rooms to accommodate visiting attorneys.

Returning to the Capitol Square one's way leads to the beautiful entrance of the Governor's Mansion.

THE GOVERNOR'S MANSION

Capitol Square · No. 3 on Richmond map

THIS CHARMING old residence, in the northeast corner of the Capitol Square was erected under an act of February 13, 1811, signed by Governor James Monroe. The "Mansion," as it is styled, was built on the site of the original wooden residence of the Chief Executive, and was completed by 1813. James Barbour was the first Governor to occupy the structure. It remained structurally unchanged till 1906, when the present dining-room in the rear of the original building was added. In all the vicissitudes of long occupancy, the Mansion has suffered little damage. The only disaster of consequence occurred December, 1925, when during a children's party, the Christmas tree caught fire. The fire spread through the interior of the residence, damaged several valuable paintings and marred many pieces of furniture. At once the house was restored and was refurnished with antiques and authentic reproductions.

With few exceptions, Richmond's distinguished guests have at one time or another, been entertained at the Mansion by the various governors. One of the most brilliant affairs, attended by prominent society was a sumptuous banquet given by Governor James Pleasants, Junior, in honor of Lafayette.

During the sad days of the War Between the States, the Mansion was a more sombre residence. After the tragic death of General Stonewall Jackson, his body was brought here where it remained overnight, before it was placed in the House of Delegates of the Capitol. Later, while the city was under martial rule, the Mansion was occupied by Brigadier-General Devens. With this exception, only the Governors of Virginia have resided in the Mansion.

THE WASHINGTON MONUMENT

Capitol Square · No. 4 on Richmond map

WALKING WEST from the Governor's Mansion, one views the equestrian statue of George Washington, which of the four monuments in Capitol Square, is the largest, the earliest and most renowned. In 1849, the Virginia Historical Society appointed a committee to solicit of the Legislature an appropriation for a monument to be erected to General Washington in the Capitol Square. The hope was, that if Mount Vernon passed from the Washington family into other private hands, the body of the "Father of His Country" would be reinterred under an impressive monument.

A bill was passed in 1849 to erect this memorial at a cost of one hundred thousand dollars. The commission was awarded to Thomas Crawford, then the most eminent of American sculptors. The following winter the site was selected and the cornerstone was laid. Crawford went to Vienna to make his models and to supervise the casting. Tradition has it that the bronze for the equestrian figure of Washington came from melted-down cannon that had been used to defend Vienna from the Turks. This figure was unveiled in 1858 with appropriate ceremonies. A few aged survivors of the Revolution were among the thousands who attended the exercises.

Due to the unfortunate and early death of Thomas Crawford, the sculptor, the work was completed by Randolph Rogers. Before his death, Crawford had finished all the models except the statues of Lewis and Nelson and the trophies. The pedestal and base were the work of Robert Mills, architect of the United States Treasury building, Washington.

The bronze figures surrounding the base of the monument are listed in order of their erection: Thomas Jefferson, Patrick Henry, George Mason, John Marshall, Andrew Lewis, Thomas Nelson. The lower symbolic groups represent "Justice and Retribution," "Colonial Times and the Bill of Rights," "Finance" and "Independence."

THE BELL TOWER

Capitol Square · No. 5 on Richmond map

DESCENDING a slight incline from the Washington Monument one reaches, on the Ninth Street side of the Capitol Square facing West Franklin Street, the time worn brick bell tower which was built in 1824. It is on the site of an ancient Guard-house, which from Mordecai's description of "Richmond in By-Gone Days," did not enhance the beauty of the Square. "The belfry, now rather disfiguring the square, was preceded by a much uglier edifice: a shabby, old second-hand wooden house, occupied as barracks by the Public Guard . . . The grounds immediately around it were bedecked with the shirts of the soldiers and the chemises of their wives, which flaunted on clothes-lines, and pigs, poultry and children enlivened the scene." The bell in the old wooden predecessor, long warned the early inhabitants of approaching danger. In peace time it rang for festive and funereal occasions and as a fire alarm for the volunteer fire department and bucket brigade. During the wars of 1812 and 1861, the clanging of the ancient bell summoned the soldiers to defend the city. Today, its years of usefulness ended, the restored bell tower stands peacefully amid beautiful trees on the grassy slope, viewing the ever changing course of progress.

ST. PAUL'S EPISCOPAL CHURCH

Grace and Ninth Streets · No. 6 on Richmond map

LEAVING THE Capitol Square by way of the Grace Street entrance gate and crossing Ninth Street, one is in front of St. Paul's Episcopal Church. The cornerstone of this historic church was laid on October 10, 1843, by Bishop John Johns. Two years later the church was consecrated. Thomas S. Stewart, of Philadelphia, the architect, modelled the edifice after St. Luke's Church in Philadelphia. Despite its age, this edifice is the largest Episcopal Church in Richmond and still is attended by many of the most prominent people of the city. Here, in 1859 was held the first Virginia meeting of the General Convention of the Episcopal Church in America. As if to foreshadow the evil days that were ahead, John Brown's raid on Harper's Ferry occured while this convention was sitting. After the removal of the Southern capitol to Richmond in May, 1861, St. Paul's became the "court church of the Confederacy." Often the President and as many as twenty Confederate Generals were to be counted among the worshipers. On the beautiful spring morning of April 2, 1865, during the regular service, a messenger entered the church and went to the pew which President Davis occupied. He whispered a message which prompted Mr. Davis to rise and quietly to follow him out. The message was that the lines in front of Petersburg had been broken and that Richmond must be evacuated. These years are eternity. Silently one stands amid sacred surroundings. Over the altar is an exquisite mosaic of Leonardo da Vinci's Last Supper, through the rich tones of the stained glass windows sunbeams catch and reflect rainbow hues across the white marble aisle.

THE JOHN MARSHALL HOUSE

Marshall and Ninth Streets · No. 7 on Richmond map

DRIVING NORTH on Ninth Street for two blocks one reaches Marshall Street where, on the northwest corner, stands the John Marshall House. This lovely old residence was built about 1790 for John Marshall, who then was practicing law in Richmond. His family was residing here when, in 1801, he was made Chief Justice of the Supreme Court of the United States. In the rooms of this dwelling he pondered and developed many of the principles enunciated in his famous opinions. Although he first saw light in Fauquier County, fought with Washington in several of the colonies, studied law in Williamsburg and subsequently presided over courts held in many cities, John Marshall regarded Richmond as his "home town." In almost every civic enterprise, to the end of his days, he had a generous and usually a directing hand. After his death in Philadelphia, July 6, 1835, his body was brought to this house prior to its interment beside his wife in interesting old Shockoe Cemetery, which lies at the north end of Third Street. The dwelling had many subsequent occupants until, in 1911, it was acquired by the City of Richmond as part of the tract purchased for a new high school. Appropriately enough, the School was named after Marshall, and the old house was entrusted to the Association for the Preservation of Virginia Antiquities. By that organization it has been restored and is now used as a depository for relics of its great first owner. Here, along with his books and some of his furniture, may be seen one of the robes Marshall wore as Chief Justice.

THE VALENTINE MUSEUM

1009-1015 East Clay Street   ·   No. 8 on Richmond map

CONTINUING NORTH on Ninth Street one block to Clay Street and turning right, one sees at the end of the square the Valentine Museum. The building which originally housed the museum was erected in 1812. Robert Mills, a distinguished architect, designed the house for John Wickham, who was a prominent member of the Richmond Bar and counsel for Aaron Burr in the trial for treason. During the War Between the States, Charles Gustavus Memminger, the Confederate Secretary of the Treasury, occupied the house. In the early eighties, Mann Satterwhite Valentine, the second, bought the property from James G. Brooks. Upon Mr. Valentine's death in 1892, he bequeathed the building to the City of Richmond as a public museum. With it he left his art collection and library. To these were added many Virginia Indian antiquities as the gift of his sons, Granville Gray, Mann Satterwhite, the third, Edward Pleasants and Benjamin Batchelder Valentine, who, with their father, had spent years in accumulating them. The contents of the Museum increased to such an extent that the original building could no longer display them adequately. In 1928 the Trustees acquired the three adjoining houses, remodelled them as a unit and removed the art, archaeological and ethnological collections into them. There the collections are assembled in such a way that they record the history of culture retrospectively. The story is begun on the first floor with present-day Virginia culture as exemplified by the work of Edward Virginius Valentine, is carried through the European Renaissance, through the Classic Age of Greece and Rome, is related to the older civilizations of Egypt, the Tigris-Euphrates and the Far East, and is traced back to primitive man in Europe, in the South Seas, in Africa and in North America. The mansion, which had been the museum's original home, is now treated as part of the general plan.

Regretfully leaving the spacious rooms of this dignified residence, one strolls across the curved, pillared portico into its peaceful and inviting garden, where an ancient magnolia and a towering tulip poplar shade the moss-covered fountain. Following the box-bordered pathway, one faces Valentine's Studio.

VALENTINE'S STUDIO

Garden of the Valentine Museum

1009-1015 East Clay Street · No. 8 on Richmond map

IN THE REAR of the museum annex and facing the garden of the old Wickham-Valentine House stands the stucco studio of Edward Virginius Valentine. Born in Richmond in 1838, his boyhood was spent with his parents, Mr. and Mrs. Mann Satterwhite Valentine, the first. At the early age of nineteen he went abroad where he studied art in Paris, Berlin and Florence, returning shortly after the close of the War Between the States.

In 1871 he bought an old stable on the south side of Leigh Street between Eighth and Ninth, then a popular but now deserted street. This he converted into his studio which he occupied as a workshop for the rest of his career as a sculptor. It was in this studio that Valentine modelled his recumbent statue of General Lee in the Lee Chapel at Washington and Lee University, Lexington, Virginia, the Thomas Jefferson statue in the Jefferson Hotel in this city, the Hugh Mercer monument at Fredericksburg, Virginia, and the statue of General Robert E. Lee in the Capitol at Washington.

When his hands could no longer mold the clay or chisel the marble, he turned to a study of the old court records and historical data of the city of Richmond. These notes and extracts have been filed at the Valentine Museum, where they are available to students and persons interested in the history of this city.

At Mr. Valentine's death in 1930, his studio, unused for several years, had not been abandoned or dismantled. Therefore when in 1936 the city of Richmond condemned this and near by property to make way for a drill ground and athletic field for the John Marshall High School, the Trustees of the Valentine Museum agreed to maintain the studio if the city would pay the cost of its removal to the garden of the Valentine Museum. The Common Council passed an appropriate ordinance, and in the spring of 1937 the old studio was opened at its new location.

54

MATTHEW FONTAINE MAURY HOUSE

1105 East Clay Street · No. 9 on Richmond map

RELUCTANTLY LEAVING the charming old garden of the Wickham-Valentine House, one proceeds east to the middle of the block where, on the right hand side of the street, one pauses to read an inconspicuous tablet on the old Maury residence. The only claim to fame of this house of the early forties is that during the early part of the War Between the States, Matthew Fontaine Maury lived here. Maury is one of the greatest yet most neglected Americans, the "Path-finder of the Seas." During his residence here, with his cousin, Robert H. Maury, he made his first experiments on submarine electric torpedoes. Nothing has been done to preserve this house and were it not for the small marker on the front wall, it would pass unnoticed.

THE CONFEDERATE MUSEUM

"The White House of the Confederacy"

Twelfth and Clay Streets · No. 10 on Richmond map

CONTINUING TO the corner, one parks, then crosses
Twelfth Street and enters the stately old "White House of the Confederacy." This house was built after plans by Robert Mills for Doctor
John Brockenbrough and his wife, Gabriella Harvie, in 1818. James
Morson, who bought the property from Doctor Brockenbrough, added
the third floor, stuccoed the building and put in the Carara marble
mantel-pieces. Later he sold the residence to James Seddon, Secretary
of War of the Confederate States.

When Richmond became the Capital of the Con-
federacy, the City bought, furnished and offered this house to the President and Mrs. Davis. The gift was declined, but the Confederate Government rented the property as an Executive Mansion. Mrs. Davis
confided that she would have preferred a house with more rooms, less
large, but she made the best of the vast chambers, and entertained
with fine hospitality. Frequent levees, open to the public, were held.
Virtually all the public officials and most of the Generals of the Army
of Northern Virginia came often to the mansion, which sometimes was
called the "Gray House of the Confederacy" to distinguish it from the
White House in Washington. A small guard of invalided soldiers gave
to the place a martial air, accentuated by the frequent arrival of couriers.

Not until the fall of 1870 was the house returned
to the city. Converted soon into a Public School, the Mansion was used
for that purpose until 1894, when the municipality gave the premises
to the Confederate Memorial Literary Society for use as a Confederate
Museum. Two years later it was opened to the public. Each state of
the Confederacy is represented by a room which contains its own
relics. Among these priceless treasures are the Original Great Seal of
the Confederate States of America, the Provisional Constitution of the
Confederate States and the sword of General Robert E. Lee.

In the yard of the Museum is the propeller shaft
of the "Virginia-Merrimac," the "first of the ironclads."

58

THE MEDICAL COLLEGE OF VIRGINIA

Marshall and College Streets · No. 11 on Richmond map

HEADING SOUTH from Twelfth and Clay Streets, one drives one block to Marshall Street, turns left and at the next corner is the interesting old Medical College of Virginia. In tribute to the contributions made by the ancient Egyptians to the "healing art," Thomas S. Stewart gave to the main building of the Medical Department of Hampden-Sidney College the architecture of the Nile when, in 1845, he designed the structure at College and Marshall Streets. As the name indicated, the institution was an offspring of Hampden-Sidney College, in Prince Edward County, which, in 1838, had opened a medical school in the old Union Hotel, Nineteenth and Main Streets. In 1854 the Medical College of Virginia became a separate corporation. It received a notable accession of students in 1859, when Southerners who were studying their profession in Philadelphia "seceded" as a result of the John Brown Raid and came en masse to Richmond. During the War Between the States, though many of its leading teachers were with the army or in the city's vast hospitals, the Medical College continued to train surgeons for the military establishment of the Confederacy. Today the great buildings of the Medical College surround the old "Egyptian Building," but it is the seal and symbol of a hundred years of service and is preserved with reverent care through the generosity of Mr. Bernard M. Baruch, who has recently restored and remodeled the ancient edifice.

FIRST AFRICAN BAPTIST CHURCH

College and Broad Streets · *No. 12 on Richmond map*

ACROSS THE STREET from the old Egyptian Building, on the northeast corner of College and Broad Streets, is the time-worn First African Baptist Church. Here was the cradle of the Baptist faith in Richmond. Following the pioneer labors in the city of Joshua Morris, a meeting house, with Reverend John Courtney as elder, was established in 1800 on Cary Street between Second and Third. After the elapse of a few years, the First Baptist Church in Richmond was built on land given by Doctor Philip Turpin at the corner of College and Broad Streets, near the "Old Richmond Theatre." In 1838, the congregation consisting of both white and colored persons, decided to separate. The old church was turned over to the colored members and became known as The First African Baptist Church. A new church for the white congregation was reared at Twelfth and Broad Streets.

The original First African Baptist Church, of cruciform design, was used for thirty years both for religious services and for public meetings, patriotic and political. Confederate leaders and Radicals of the reconstruction era thundered their appeals within these walls. In 1876 the old church was demolished and the present building erected. Since the close of the War Between the States, when the first Negro minister was chosen, the church has had only three pastors.

MONUMENTAL EPISCOPAL CHURCH

Broad near College Street · No. 13 on Richmond map

LEAVING THE historic African Church, one walks across College Street and half a block up Broad Street hill to the hallowed ground of Monumental Episcopal Church. Here, on the night after Christmas, 1811, the Placide Stock Company was presenting in the Theatre on Shockoe Hill "The Father Or Family Feuds" and Louis Hue Girardin's translation of one of Diderot's plays, "Raymond and Agnes or the Bleeding Nun." During the second act of a crowded performance a candle set fire to a hanging scene. In a few minutes the entire building was ablaze. When the fire had burnt itself out, a count of the stricken audience showed that seventy persons had perished. The newly-elected Governor, George W. Smith and a former United States Senator, Abram B. Venable, were among the victims.

The site had been that of the Virginia Academy, in which the Convention of 1788 had discussed the ratification of the Constitution of 1787. After the holocaust of 1811, Richmond decided to erect on the ground a Memorial Church. As architect Robert Mills, of South Carolina, was chosen. On August 1, 1812, the cornerstone was laid, and with funds raised publicly, the edifice was reared. In the late spring of 1814 the church was opened for the first time. The Reverend Richard Channing Moore, of New York City, became the first rector of the church and while ministering there, served as Bishop of the Diocese of Virginia. The building, which is well worth inspection, was one of several designed by Robert Mills during his stay in Richmond prior to the time when he was Engineer and Architect of his native State, South Carolina, and before he received the commission for the Obelisk, the famous Washington Monument.

THE MASONIC HALL

1805 East Franklin Street · *No. 14 on Richmond map*

TAKING LEAVE of Court End of town and heading for old Richmond and the Tobacco District, one drives east on Broad Street to Fourteenth Street, turns right, and continues south two blocks to Franklin Street. Here, turn left and drive through the "Old Market," where picturesque covered-wagons flank the uneven brick sidewalks, to 1805 East Franklin Street, the oldest Masonic Hall, built and used as such, in the United States.

A public lottery supplied funds for this Masonic Hall, which was begun in 1785, on land purchased from Gabriel Galt. The Hall was occupied two years later by Richmond-Randolph Lodge, No. 19, which still holds its meetings there. So long an occupancy has brought within the doors of the lodge many notable Masons, among them the Marquis de Lafayette and his son, who was named after George Washington. In their honor was given a dinner, over which Chief Justice John Marshall, Master of Richmond Lodge No. 10, presided. War and men of arms have played no small part in the history of the Hall. It was used as a military hospital during the war of 1812, and later was visited by many Confederate and Federal officers. One Union Mason, attending a Lodge meeting soon after the close of the war, forgetfully left his sword in the building. It is still there.

POE FOUNDATION INCORPORATED

1916 East Main Street · No. 15 on Richmond map

CONTINUING EAST on Franklin Street to Twentieth Street, turn right and drive one block to Main Street, turn right and park. In the middle of the square on the same side of the street is "The Old Stone House," now the Poe Foundation. Perhaps because of the material used for its construction, "The Old Stone House" has survived all the early dwellings of Richmond. It is thought to have been built prior to 1737, and is known to have been used a few years later as the residence of Jacob Ege, a native of Germany. During the Revolutionary War Samuel Ege, a commissary in the American Army and grandson of the original owner, occupied the house. It was at this time, as legends run, that many famous Americans visited the premises, but of none of these associations is there any record. The tradition which caused the house to be styled "Washington's Headquarters" is certainly unfounded, as Washington never maintained military headquarters in Richmond. The first newspaper published in Richmond after the War Between the States was issued here by a Federal officer. Thereafter the house had numerous tenants unknown to fame, and it became, in time, a souvenir store. In 1922, it was set aside as a Shrine to Edgar Allan Poe, not because he ever lived here, but because the building was one of comparatively few that retained substantially the appearance it had in the years when Poe lived in Richmond. The Poe Foundation here houses its notable collection of books, periodicals, and manuscripts. Here, also, are Poe's trunk and other relics of his life.

The "enchanted Garden" in rear of the story-and-a-half stone house has many furnishings from old streets and buildings that Poe knew. Against the back wall stands a pergola made of stone and brick from the old building of the Southern Literary Messenger, which Poe edited in 1835-37. The original offices of the Messenger, at the southeast corner of Fifteenth and Main Street, have been demolished.

Across from the garden in a modern brick building, which is a copy of an old dwelling on lower Main Street, the most valuable collections of the Poe Foundation are on display.

ADAM CRAIG HOUSE

1812 East Grace Street · No. 16 on Richmond map

HAVING DREAMED with Poe for a few short moments, one desires to see some tangible reality of his beautiful "Helen." This is found at her birthplace only a few squares away. Driving west one and a half blocks to Eighteenth Street, one turns right and drives north for two more blocks and turns right on Grace Street where immediately the restored home of Jane Craig is in full view.

Tradition dates this old two story clapboard house 1770. The records show that from 1790 to 1822 it was owned and occupied by Adam Craig, Clerk of Hustings Court, a leading citizen and the father of Jane Stith Craig, Poe's immortal "Helen." Jane Craig was born and lived here until her marriage to Judge Robert Stanard.

After the War Between the States, this was the residence of James Shields, long a prominent citizen and the last private owner.

The Association for the Preservation of Virginia Antiquities obtained this historic house in 1935, from the Trinity Institutional Church and has restored the dwelling and garden. The premises now are used as a modern Negro Art Center.

ST. JOHN'S EPISCOPAL CHURCH

2400 East Broad Street · No. 17 on Richmond map

AT THE CORNER of Nineteenth and Grace Streets one turns right to Franklin Street. Here turn left and drive east for two blocks, passing, on the right, between Twentieth and Twenty-first Streets the First Jewish Cemetery in Virginia. This ancient enclosed burying ground, long since abandoned, was dedicated in 1791. At the corner of Twenty-first Street turn left to Broad Street, make a right turn and drive east until reaching Twenty-fourth Street and historic St. John's Episcopal Church.

Richmond's oldest house of worship, the only one that dates from the eighteenth century, was known at the time of its erection, about 1741, simply as the "New Church," or "Town Church" and was built on ground set aside for the purpose when the town of Richmond was laid out by direction of William Byrd, the second, of "Westover." Since 1829 "New Church" has been known as St. John's Church, Henrico Parish. The Reverend William Stith, author of "The History of Virginia" and one time President of William and Mary College, was the first rector. In the original church, which constitutes the transepts of the present enlarged building, met the Virginia Convention of March, 1775. On the third day of this Convention, Patrick Henry spoke in behalf of the resolution to arm the Colony. He concluded with the historic appeal: "Is life so dear or peace so sweet as to be purchased at the price of chains and slavery? Forbid it, Almighty God! I know not what course others may take, but as for me, give me liberty or give me death!" The tradition is that he stood then in the pew now numbered 47. His place is shown to visitors, as is the seventeenth-century baptismal bowl from long-vanished Curles Neck Church. The bell of St. John's, believed to be that used in 1775, is now in the home of the Virginia Historical Society.

During the brief British occupation of Richmond in 1781, Benedict Arnold's troops used the church as barracks. After the Revolution, the Rector was Reverend John Buchanan, a unique character whose personality and devoted service are recorded in "The Two Parsons," by George Wythe Munford.

73

THE VIRGINIA HISTORICAL SOCIETY

707 East Franklin Street · No. 18 on Richmond map

LEAVING THE peaceful solemnity of old St. John's, one's journey leads back to the bustle and din of the business section of the city. Heading west on Broad Street, one continues until reaching Eighth Street, here turn left, drive south for two blocks and turn right at Franklin Street, where, in the middle of the block on the south side of the street, is the part-time war residence of Mrs. Robert E. Lee, now the Virginia Historical Society.

When Richmond's population of 37,000 was swollen during the War Between the States to a restless 100,000, some of the aides of President Davis considered themselves fortunate to be able to establish themselves in this ample house, which was one in a distinguished row built by Norman Stewart in 1844. About January, 1864, for a variety of reasons, "The Mess," as it was styled in strict military parlance, broke up. Its members gallantly offered their lease to Mrs. Robert E. Lee, wife of the commander of the Army of Northern Virginia. She occupied the house until June, 1865, when she left Richmond. It was in this house that General Lee pondered his ever-increasing problems during his visits to Richmond in the winter of 1864-65; and it was to this haven that he returned after Appomattox. The stone steps that he mounted and the door that he closed behind him when he "unbelted his sword forever" remain as they were in 1865. The house, for more than forty years, has been the home of the Virginia Historical Society, which was organized December 29, 1831. The valuable belongings of the Society, including many items of unique historical interest, are displayed in the old residence and in the modern rear annex.

PRATT'S CASTLE

Gambles Hill

South End of Fourth Street · *No. 19 on Richmond map*

CONTINUING WEST on Franklin Street to Fourth Street, turn left and drive to its terminus. Here one pauses to view the pseudo-castle which is credited with a secret room and a dungeon. It is of no historical value, but architecturally it is a most interesting example of the influence on Virginia of the Gothic romanticism that ran rampant from Strawberry Hill through the pages of Ann Radcliffe and overflowed into the poems of Byron. Virginia so thrilled to that romanticism that W. A. Pratt, of Whitehurst and Pratt, one of the first daguerrean artists in Richmond, built this "Gothic Residence" in the eighteen fifties and later offered it as the capital prize in a lottery among his customers. In time, "Pratt's Castle" passed to the late Joseph F. Biggs, who furnished it with Early American antiques and for a while opened it to the public. It is now the private home of his widow.

HOME OF ELLEN GLASGOW

One West Main Street · *No. 20 on Richmond map*

BEFORE PURSUING one's journey, circle around Gamble's Hill where, on its commanding site instead of at the real landing at the falls on the rocks of the Lower James, is erected a cross in memory of Captains Newport and Smith and their band of twenty-one men who, in June, 1607, first set foot on land at the Falls and there set up a cross. On the southern bank of the muddy James is old Manchester, now South Richmond. On the east, at the foot of several terraces, is the Tredegar Iron Works, established in 1836. Looking west, in the distance is Hollywood, Richmond's first private cemetery, which is considered one of the most beautiful in this country. There rest many heroes, famous statesmen and prominent citizens. A few among the many notables are two Presidents of the United States, James Monroe and John Tyler; the only President of the Confederacy, Jefferson Davis; the "Pathfinder of the Seas," Matthew Fontaine Maury, and General J. E. B. Stuart.

Leaving Gamble's Hill by way of Third Street, one heads north until reaching Main Street; here turn left and drive two blocks where in passing one views the old Crozet House, built in 1814 by Curtis Carter but unreclaimed until 1940; continue to Foushee Street where, on the southwest corner, stands the stately gray stucco residence of Ellen Anderson Glasgow, the novelist. Surrounding it are rundown former homes of the elite, modern garages and antique shops, but even these do not detract from the charm of the lovely prewar dwelling with its wrought iron fence and steep stone steps. A beautiful magnolia and evergreens shade the entrance, while in the rear, hidden behind a high picket fence, is a peaceful, old-fashion garden. Within its dignified walls resides the charming Virginia authoress who gives to the world such books as "They Stoop to Folly," "The Sheltered Life" and "Vein of Iron." The house was built in 1842 by David M. Branch. Within the next four years it was the home of Isaac Davenport, merchant and banker, whose daughter sold it in 1887 to Francis Glasgow, the father of the present owner.

REVEILLE

Cary Street Road · No. 21 on Richmond map

ONE TURNS to the right at Foushee Street, which is the dividing line of East and West Richmond, drives one block to Franklin Street, turns left and keeps straight ahead. Franklin Street, with its lovely arching trees which in the spring meet over head, is the city's late nineteenth and early twentieth century fashionable residential section. A few squares farther is Monroe Park, in 1854 the State Fair grounds and later Camp Lee for Confederate soldiers. One arrives next at the (J. E. B.) Stuart Monument by Fred Moynihan. At this intersection Franklin Street becomes Monument Avenue and, as its name implies, is an avenue of memorials. One pauses in passing to view each. At Allen Avenue is the equestrian statue of General Lee by Jean Antoine Mercié. Then comes the imposing monument in honor of President Davis by Edward V. Valentine, followed in order by the two beautiful statues of "Stonewall" Jackson and Matthew Fontaine Maury, both by William Sievers, of Richmond. Circling the Maury monument, one returns to the equestrian Jackson at the Boulevard and turns right to Cary Street. Before reaching Cary Street, one passes the Confederate Memorial Institute (Battle Abbey), the Confederate Soldiers' Home and the Virginia Museum of Fine Arts. Turning right at Cary Street and the Boulevard, driving west for several blocks and crossing the bridge one is no longer within the city limits. Less than half a mile, on the right hand side of the road, almost concealed by a high evergreen hedge and towering trees, is "Reveille," a private residence and therefore not open to visitors.

This beautiful old rambling, gabled-roofed dwelling is one of the earliest in or near Richmond. Prior to 1791, when the original part was built, the estate was referred to as "the old Brick House Tract." Although not recorded as such until 1852, tradition says it received its present name during the Revolutionary War. Reveille changed hands countless times until after the War Between the States, when it became the home of Doctor R. A. Patterson, whose daughter, Mrs. E. Mulford Crutchfield, now owns and occupies it.

Reveille contains a rare collection of antiques and is surrounded by a spacious lawn, old trees and the loveliest of gardens.

WILTON

Wilton Road by way of Cary Street Road

No. 22 on Richmond map

PASSING REVEILLE and continuing west for one mile, one turns left on Wilton Road at an historical marker, "Wilton," where at the foot of a steep hill in a beautiful grove of trees is the stately mansion. Virginians cherish their old sites almost as much as they love their old homes; but sometimes, if they must leave the sites, they move the homes. Wilton is a case in point. The house was built about six miles down the James River from Richmond on land known as "World's End," in 1753 by William Randolph, the third, son of William Randolph, the second, of Turkey Island, Henrico County. At his death, his son, Peyton Randolph, inherited the property. It was also the home of Anne Randolph, sister of Peyton, known as "Nancy Wilton," the belle and beauty. In her train of admirers were Thomas Jefferson, later to become President of the United States; John Page, a future Governor of Virginia; and Benjamin Harrison of Brandon, Prince George County. Benjamin Harrison was the man of her choice. Wilton remained in the Randolph family until the War Between the States. At this time, Mrs. Edward C. Mayo, daughter of Peyton Randolph, sold the estate to Colonel William Carter Knight, during whose occupancy Wilton was the scene of endless activity.

In time, Colonel Knight sold the estate to George Cornwall. Subsequently the place changed hands several times.

In 1933, the house was bought by the Virginia Society of the Colonial Dames of America, who have moved and rebuilt it on a bluff overlooking the upper James River, off Cary Street Road. Wilton today is one of the most interesting reconstructed residences in Virginia and is unique in that the original wood is used throughout its spacious halls, eight beautifully proportioned rooms and even in the closets which are panelled from floor to ceiling in heart pine. Visitors are welcome on week days from nine in the morning to five in the afternoon and on Sunday from nine to twelve in the morning and from three to six in the afternoon.

AMPTHILL HOUSE

Ampthill Road, by way of Cary Street Road

No. 23 on Richmond map

DEPARTING FROM the charm of Wilton, one follows the road on the right up the incline and turns south on Ampthill Road. At the foot of the hill, on the left, is the entrance to Ampthill House, the reconstructed ancestral residence of the Cary family. This beautiful old salmon colored brick house originally stood on the bank of the James River, west of Falling Creek in Chesterfield County where today, on its site, flourishes the cellophane division of the E. I. DuPont de Nemours and Company, Incorporated.

Henry Cary, son of Miles Cary, was the first owner of Ampthill plantation but it was his son, Henry, who in 1732 built the dwelling. Both of the Henry Carys were experienced builders of their day. They had superintended the erection of the Capitol at Williamsburg and later, after the fire, the rebuilding of the William and Mary College.

It was not until the "small and fiery, quick-tempered and tempestuous" Archibald Cary inherited the estate that it was called Ampthill. He married the lovely Mary Randolph of "old" Wilton on the lower James, then across the river and now again a near neighbor.

Following the Cary ownership, the property passed to the Temple and the Watkin families. Finally, after years of neglect, the staunch old house fell into a sad state of dilapidation.

In 1929, Hunsdon Cary, Esquire, a direct descendant of the first owner, acquired Ampthill, which under his and Mrs. Cary's careful supervision, has been rebuilt amid harmonious surroundings.

AGECROFT HALL

Windsor Farms, Cary Street Road · No. 24 on Richmond map

RELUCTANTLY taking leave of Ampthill House and its beautiful setting, one retraces the way to Cary Street Road, turns right and continues east for about a mile to Windsor Farms, a modern but lovely residential development. Entering by Coventry Road, one turns right at Nottingham Road, continuing on same until reaching Sulgrave Road, here turn left to the stately iron entrance gate of Agecroft Hall. The original site of ancient Agecroft Manor House was a bleak district on the Irewell, in Lancashire, England. The Manor House had belonged to the Langleys, who were of the royal Plantagenets, and it contained interesting architectural examples of the manner in which pre-Elizabethan dwellings were enlarged during prosperous generations into rambling courts that housed many retainers. The late Mr. Thomas C. Williams purchased Agecroft in 1925 and removed the more substantial parts to the vicinity of Richmond, where the noble old timbered house was reconstructed with a garden that suggests Hampton Court. Under the terms of Mr. Williams' bequest, Agecroft ultimately will become a museum for the City of Richmond. The residence is privately occupied by Dr. and Mrs. David Morton, therefore neither it nor the extensive grounds are open to visitors.

VIRGINIA HOUSE

Windsor Farms, Cary Street Road · *No. 25 on Richmond map*

ADJOINING Agecroft Hall is another interesting reconstructed English manor house. To save the ancient Priory of the Holy Sepulcher at Warwick, England, from demolition, Mr. and Mrs. Alexander W. Weddell purchased the structure and shipped it to Richmond. Near the city in Windsor Farms, overlooking the James River, the present Virginia House was constructed in 1925. "The main body of Virginia House is after the Tudor portion of the Priory; the wing west of the main entrance door is a copy of the principal part of the original structure of Sulgrave Manor, the English home of the ancestors of George Washington; the entrance tower is a reproduction of the one at Wormleighton, another English home associated with the Washingtons through their intermarriage with the Spencers." In 1929 Mr. and Mrs. Weddell, who retained a life interest, conveyed Virginia House to the Virginia Historical Society as its future home. Adjacent to the mansion is a garden of the four seasons. Like all private residences, they are closed to visitors except on stated occasions when a sign at their entrances will give this information. Leaving Virginia House and continuing on Sulgrave Road one turns right with the ivy covered serpentine wall on Storkton Lane to the Oaks. This ancient dwelling originally stood on land owned by Benjamin Harrison, the fourth, in Amelia County. There is no recorded date of its construction but the year accepted is 1745. Today, amid congenial surroundings but still unpainted the silver hues of the clapboards add unusual charm. The interior contains beautiful panelling, fine carved mantels and interesting old wooden-pegged, pine doors. Having driven slightly over four miles since entering Windsor Farms, one heads north to Cary Street Road and turns right to Richmond and one's place of abode.

OLD INDIAN TRAIL

"OLD INDIAN TRAIL"

Route 5

STARTING AGAIN from the entrance of the Capitol Square, Grace and Ninth Streets, one drives south on Ninth Street to Main Street, turns left and continues east through the financial and the industrial district of the city to Twenty-eighth Street, where from the foot of Libby Hill Park, one may glimpse the Soldiers' and Sailors' Monument, the work of William Sheppard, a native of Richmond. Here one follows Williamsburg Avenue to Route 5 or "Old Indian Trail." From Richmond, our pilgrimage carries us down the "Peninsula of Virginia" on the north side of James river, through the counties of Henrico and Charles City and past many renowned estates. The present Highway, No. 5, probably follows approximately the course of "The Old Indian Trail," which doubtless is one of the most ancient travelways in the United States. From the road, which is hard-surfaced for the entire distance, the traveler sees a pleasant countryside, devoted in the main to dairies and to the growing of grain; but if he turns off the highway to almost any grove, he is apt to find an old house, and if he wanders into the woods he is likely to discover overgrown earthworks. For this was in the sixties one of the great battlegrounds of fratercidal strife, the remains of which are visible on almost every eminence and by the sides of many of the roads and streams. The chief engagements in this area were in July, 1862, and again in the long operations that began with Grant's crossing of the James, June, 1864, and ended with the evacuation of the Richmond-Petersburg defenses, April 2-3, 1865. In few parts of America are the grim evidences of the War between the States brought into such juxtaposition to the spacious, the baronial mansions of the eighteenth century. Even the names echo both eras. Malvern Hill is at once the site of a great battle (July 1, 1862) and of a seventeenth-century home, the foundations of which alone survive. Turkey Island recalls a famous family and a great bombardment. Westover was one of the greatest estates of Virginia in the days of William Byrd the second—and was within the frowning enclosure of the defensive works that General McClellan occupied around Harrison's Landing after his retreat from Malvern Hill. It is a country through which to pass slowly . . . and reverently.

93

TREE HILL

Old Indian Trail · Route 5, Henrico County

THE FIRST place of interest on Old Indian Trail is a fraction over four miles from the Capitol to its entrance and back to the highway. The center and original part of this clapboard dwelling is two stories high and square with four white-washed brick chimneys. One story wings and porches now add to its usefulness and symmetry. The date of its erection is unknown, but before 1811 it was the residence of Colonel Miles Cary Selden. Tree Hill, in the early eighteen hundreds, was one of the most noted racing centers in America. It was here, in one of the events staged in honor of Lafayette, that "Virginia," a famous mare, owned by William R. Johnson, of Chesterfield County, Virginia, won an historic race.

During the War Between the States, the owner, Franklin Stearns, loaned this celebrated farm to the Chimborazo Hospital for the pasturage for hundreds of goats. The young meat of these prolific animals proved "a most palatable and nutritious food for the sick and convalescent patients." It was not far below Tree Hill that Mayor Joseph Mayo, with a committee, surrendered the city of Richmond to the Federals—surrendered it, tradition says, with a torn shirt-tail as no flag of truce was at hand.

The present owner of Tree Hill, W. J. Burlee, inherited the property from his uncle.

VARINA

Old Indian Trail · *Route 5, Henrico County*

CONTINUING a little over half a mile, one passes the Virginia Historical Marker giving directions to the original site of Wilton, now reconstructed, amid harmonious surroundings, on Wilton Road overlooking upper James River just outside of the western city limit of Richmond. Two miles farther is a sign marked "Richmond National Battlefield Park." If one wishes to take an additional fifteen mile drive through beautiful woods, over well cultivated land along the fertile banks of the James, to Varina, one turns right and follows closely the directions given in the list of mileage re-entering the highway about four miles south—otherwise keep straight ahead.

At "the neck of land in the upper parts," their home a small brick house, of which all traces have long since disappeared, lived the adventurous John Rolfe and his wife, the Indian Princess Pocahontas. During 1614 Rolfe began the successful cultivation of tobacco, which through the centuries has proved Virginia's most profitable agricultural industry. Twenty odd years after Rolfe's residence ended, this plantation became Varina. It was so named after the "Varina" tobacco, of Spain, which the leaf grown here resembled in flavor. Later residents added to this renown. Here lived the Reverend James Blair, rector of Varina Parish and later founder of William and Mary College, in Williamsburg; and William Stith, one time president of the college and author of a long-esteemed *History of Virginia*. During the War Between the States, this was the eastern depot for the exchange of prisoners and was known as "Aiken's Landing." Varina of today is a modern square brick house owned and occupied by Mrs. Philip N. Stoneman.

CURLES NECK

Old Indian Trail · Route 5, Henrico County

CROSSING THE concrete bridge one is in front of the main entrance to Curles Neck Farm. Originally this plantation, in one of the "curls" of James River, was divided into many small farms, but these tracts eventually were consolidated. In 1617, Edward Gurgany patented the land known as "Longfield." At his death his wife inherited it and in turn willed it to Captain Thomas Harris. Two decades later, John Pleasants, the Quaker merchant and planter, settled on Curles Neck plantation. The next in line of occupancy was Nathaniel Bacon, "the Rebel." After Bacon's uprising against a tyrannical Colonial Governor, Bacon's land was confiscated, and later was bought by William Randolph, the first, of Turkey Island, Henrico County. At one time "Bremo," the ancestral home of the Cocke family, was on Curles Neck estate. Today only tombstones mark the spot.

During the Revolution, when Lafayette's headquarters were here, Curles Neck was the residence of Ryland Randolph, grandson of William Randolph. Years later, the estate became one of the many owned by Major William Allen, of Claremont Manor, Surry County. In 1907, the property was acquired by Charles H. Senff, Esquire, the builder of the present modern brick house. He was followed by C. K. Billings. During Mr. Billings' ownership Curles Neck was the home of "Harvester," one of the most famous race horses of a generation.

The plantation is now the property of Mr. and Mrs. Albert Billings Ruddock. Through their courtesy, the annual Deep Run Hunt Club's Spring Race Meet is held here.

MALVERN HILL

Old Indian Trail · Route 5, Henrico County

A MODERN FENCE and farm road divide the prosperous farm of Curles Neck and the once renowned Turkey Island plantation. Tidal swamps, trees of dark foliage and tangled underbrush now cover much of the famous plantation, part of which belonged in 1676 to Colonial James Crews, one of the leaders in Bacon's Rebellion. After the uprising, he was hanged near Jamestown. His heirs sold the property to William Randolph, the first, son of Richard Randolph of Morton Hall, Warwickshire, England. This William Randolph was the progenitor of so many distinguished Virginians that the date of his birth has been declared one of the most important in the history of the Old Dominion. At his death, his son, William Randolph, the second, a member of the House of Burgesses, inherited the estate. Long after his day, Turkey Island plantation was on the stormy edge of the battle of Malvern Hill. At this time the old house was fired and destroyed by the gunboats in the James River. By strange irony, a section of the estate was owned at that time by General George E. Pickett, who had sustained a wound in the battle of Gaine's Mill, June 27, 1862, but survived to send his division into the famous charge at Gettysburg that made his name immortal in American history. Today, that part of Turkey Island which is not overflown by the James consists of small farms and modern residences.

A very interesting old monument was erected here after the disastrous flood of May, 1771. It bears the following inscription:

"The foundation of this pillar was laid in the calamitous year of 1771, when all the great rivers of this country were swept by inundations never before experienced, which changed the face of nature and left traces of their violence that will remain for ages."

Less than half a mile across winding old Indian Trail, on a high hill are the site and vine-covered foundation of Malvern Hills. A fancied resemblance between the high ground above Turkey Island and the historic Malvern Hills that rise from the Severn in

Worcestershire Beacon, England, led Thomas Cocke to give the old name to his new home on the James. He was the son of Richard Cocke of England, who came to Virginia in 1630 and here built a house acclaimed "one of the best specimens of Colonial architecture" in the Old Dominion. It showed definite seventeenth century influence, but, unfortunately, it was never well photographed or measured prior to its destruction by fire about 1905. James Powell Cocke sold the estate after the Revolutionary War to Robert Nelson. He was the son of Elizabeth Burwell and William Nelson, President of the Council, and was brother of General Thomas Nelson, Governor of Virginia. Subsequently, the Malvern Hills property was mortgaged to Charles Carter of Shirley, but when he died in 1806, he left specific instructions that his executors should not foreclose on the home of his friends. At that time and for at least a generation later, the name of the estate was usually in the plural—"The Malvern Hills." The singular form did not come into general use until the period of the War Between the States.

The associations of this old property are as martial as social. Lafayette encamped here for the protection of Richmond against British attack by way of the James River. In the summer of 1813, the plantation was garrisoned with several thousand men to keep the British from a similar attack. The fighting here in the great battle of July 1, 1862, occurred a slight distance to the north and northwest of the old mansion. Federal artillery was parked, hills on hills, between the Mellert (Crew) and the West Houses. The Confederate attack was southward, up the grade from Western Run. That section of the battle ground known as the "Wheatfield" lies to the west under the bluff on which the Mellert (Crew) House stands. Although Malvern Hill continued to have strategic value until it fell permanently into Federal hands in June, 1864, its later history has not been conspicuous.

CHARLES CITY COUNTY, VIRGINIA

AFTER CROSSING Turkey Island Creek, one is in Charles City County, one of the original eight shires. It was named for Charles City, at Bermuda Hundred, which was called for Charles, the First, of England. Before its division in 1702, it extended along both sides of the winding James. Today it is bounded on the south by the James and on the north and east by the Chickahominy rivers. Before 1619, three large settlements had been established, but after the Indian Massacre of 1622, they were abandoned. In less than forty-five years they were repatented and are today three beautiful estates, Westover, Shirley and Berkeley. The ninth and tenth Presidents of the United States, William Henry Harrison and John Tyler, were born in Charles City County as was John Tyler, father of the President and Governor of Virginia.

During the Revolutionary War the old county plantations were camping grounds for the British soldiers, while historic Westover Church was used as a stable for their horses. In the midwinter of 1781, Lieutenant-Colonel Simcoe and a detachment of the Queen's Rangers made a surprise attack on the old Court House. Again during the War Between the States the county was in the radius of battle with General McClellan's great Army of the Potomac established at Harrison's Landing, General Pope's headquarters at Westover and General Grant's army ferrying over James River from Wilcox Wharf to "Windmill Point" en route to Petersburg. Unique in the history of Virginia, Charles City County's white population has declined continuously since 1790.

DOGHAM

Old Indian Trail · *Route 5, Charles City County*

BETWEEN Turkey Island bridge and the entrance to Dogham one drives along the loveliest part of Old Indian Trail, which in the early spring runs riot with pure white dogwood and the mauve tints of the judas trees. The narrow private roadway leads through shady woods and a cooling stream. This land, in 1637, was a part of the eleven hundred acres granted by the King of England to Joseph Royall in consideration of the transportation of twenty persons into the colony, many of whom were of well known English families. The estate was then known as "the land on Turkey Island Creek and James River above Shirley Hundred." The adjoining tract called "Riverview Farm" was the other part of this grant, all of which was first styled Dogham, said to be a variation of "D'Aughams," the French name of a stream in Normandy.

Henry Isham, Jr. states in his will dated November 13, 1678—"I give and bequeith my plantation in Charles Citty County in Virginia . . . commonly knowne by ye name of Doggams with all the land thereto belonging, all the houses fences woods underwoods etc. to be equally divided betweene my two Sisters Mrs. Mary Randolph & Mrs. Anne Isham aforesaid to them & their heirs forever." The land and dwelling designated "Doggams," remained in the Royall family until 1928, when James Pinckney Harrison purchased the property from Mrs. William J. Hogan, nee Ida Lewis Royall, a descendant of Joseph Royall, the emigrant.

Under the supervision of Mr. and Mrs. Harrison, the quaint little story and a half white clapboard house has been restored and a story and a half addition built to form an L. The center part, which is the original, is flanked by one story wings. It nestles on the side of a hill in a grove of locust trees facing a modern but lovely, informal garden.

RIVERVIEW FARM

Old Indian Trail · Route 5, Charles City County

ADJOINING DOGHAM, and in great contrast to this charming informal dwelling, is the dignified "before the war" mansion known as Riverview. It is situated on the remaining part of the previously mentioned eleven hundred acres of land granted, in 1637, to Joseph Royall, by the King. The builder of the present house is unknown but the accepted date of its completion is 1860.

In the spring of 1936, Mr. and Mrs. Arthur J. Sackett, of New York, purchased the property from George Y. Webster in whose possession it had been for eighteen years. During the Websters' occupancy the beautiful formal garden, enclosed by an ivy covered serpentine wall, was laid out.

Architecturally, Riverview is different from any other residence along Old Indian Trail, in that it has two full stories with an attic and an English basement three steps below ground. At the time the house was remodeled, historic Westmoreland Club, in Richmond, had been demolished, to provide parking space in the shopping district, so its lovely old pine flooring was used. The two panelled basement rooms, of ancient Oregon pine, are a most inviting living room and a very attractive dining room. Across the hall is a large and comfortable guest chamber which looks out over the spacious and shady lawn to the river. Ascending the easy tread of the ground floor stairs one reaches the main or first floor where on one side of the wide hall is an enormous formal reception hall; on the other side, the master suite, bedroom, bath and study. On the third floor are four charming bedrooms, each different in color and detail.

The exterior of the English basement is of brick, plastered and painted white; the remaining part of the house is white clapboard with slate roof and soft green shutters. The pillared porches and two-storied portico add dignity and charm.

SHIRLEY

Old Indian Trail · Route 5, Charles City County

HALF A MILE from the whitewashed posts of River-view entrance, one turns right and is on the way to Shirley, one of the noblest of the old Virginia mansions and, if possible, should be seen, inside and out, by every Peninsula Pilgrim. As early as 1613, Shirley was inhabited by Englishmen and was known as West and Shirley Hundred. It was owned by Thomas West, Lord Delaware, and his brothers, Captains Francis, Nathaniel, and John West. Some forty years later the tract was patented by Colonel Edward Hill, Senior. He built "the old house," which was pulled down and rebuilt after the War Between the States, and now known as "Upper Shirley." On the death of Colonel Edward Hill, his son of the same name, sometime Treasurer of Virginia and "Commander-in-Chief of Charles City and Surry Counties," inherited Shirley. During Bacon's Rebellion the dwelling was ransacked and plundered, and Mrs. Hill and her children were made prisoners. Edward Hill, the third, builder of the present house, was a member of the House of Burgesses and Collector of the Revenue. He married Elizabeth Williams, the daughter and heiress of Sir Edward Williams, of Wales, and the owner of North Wales, Virginia. At the death of their son, Edward Hill, the fourth, a boy of sixteen, his sister, Elizabeth, inherited the plantation. She married John Carter, Secretary of State of the Colony and the son of Robert "King" Carter, of Corotoman. Since about 1740, the estate has remained in the Carter family.

Anne Hill Carter, daughter of Anne Butler Moore and Charles Carter, probably—though not certainly—was born at Shirley on March 26, 1773. Twenty years later she was married here to "Light Horse" Harry Lee. Among their children was Robert Edward Lee, who, in childhood, was a frequent visitor to the home of his mother.

Shirley is one of the few old Virginia residences that remain in the original family. One of the most interesting features of its beautiful interior is the carved walnut stair, without visible support, which starts in the square entrance hall and ascends to the third floor. The house contains antiques of various periods and valuable ancestral

portraits. The Washington portrait, by Charles Wilson Peal, now in the Capitol at Williamsburg, hung in the dining room of Shirley for over one hundred years. It was a gift from General Washington to General Nelson, and came to the Carters through Mary Nelson, daughter of General Thomas Nelson, who married Robert Carter. Their likenesses, by St. Memin, hang at Shirley on the panelled wall above the mantel in the drawing room.

Facing the big house on the land side are twin two-story brick houses, one a dwelling, the other the original kitchen and old laundry which through the long and changing years remain unaltered and daily serve their original purpose.

The estate is owned and occupied by Mrs. James Harrison Oliver, who, before her marriage to Admiral Oliver, was Miss Marion Carter.

BERKELEY

Old Indian Trail · *Route 5, Charles City County*

BACK ON old Indian Trail one drives south three miles to the highway entrance to both Berkeley and Westover. One reaches the impressive brick gates of Berkeley first. Here are the associations of a great name and the roots of great public service. Berkeley Hundred was granted February 3, 1619, by the London Company to a number of London merchants. Among them were Richard Berkeley and George Thorp. From the former of these men, the estate derives its name. Thorp, who came to Virginia to take charge of the proposed East India School and settlement, was killed in the massacre of 1622, at which time the "Town and Hundred of Berkeley" were abandoned. About fifteen years later the plantation was again patented by a merchant of London, whose son, Giles Bland, lived here. For aiding Bacon in his rebellion of 1676, the younger Bland was hanged. The estate then passed to Benjamin Harrison, the third. At his death in 1710 it was inherited by his son, Benjamin Harrison, the fourth. This Benjamin, builder of the present house, was sometime Speaker of the House of Burgesses and was the father of the "Signer." In 1727 Benjamin Harrison, the fifth to bear the name, was born here. His mother was Ann Carter, daughter of Robert Carter, of "Corotoman." Besides being a Signer of the Declaration of Independence, he was a distinguished Governor of Virginia. He married Elizabeth, daughter of Colonel William Bassett of New Kent County. Their son, William Henry Harrison, who was also born here, became the ninth president of the United States.

During the Revolutionary War, Benedict Arnold and his troops camped at Berkeley. Years later, during the War Between the States, the estate was known as Harrison's Landing. After the battle of Malvern Hill, General McClellan's great Army of the Potomac established its camp here, where it remained until August, 1862.

Berkeley of today stands proudly, surrounded by fertile fields that extend to the river's edge. It is the home of Mr. and Mrs. Malcomb Jamieson, under whose supervision it has been restored to its former beauty.

WESTOVER

Old Indian Trail · Route 5, Charles City County

RETURNING TO the entrance gate of Berkeley, one turns right and continues, through lovely wooded stretches, to Westover.

Whether Westover or Mt. Airy in Richmond County is the loveliest Colonial home of their State, Virginians often argue. The question may be one of taste, but the answer, in any case, always conceded to Westover a grace and a glory that live in the mind of every fortunate visitor. The land originally was granted to Captain Francis West in 1619, for Henry West, son and heir of Lord Delaware, Governor of Virginia. It was for him that Westover was named. Captain Thomas Pawlett, brother of Lord Pawlett, patented part of this land in 1637. In less than ten years Lord Pawlett fell heir to his brother's plantation. He sold it to Theodorick Bland, brother to John Bland, London merchant, whose son lived at Berkeley. When Theodorick Bland died, his heirs sold the property to William Byrd, the first, Receiver-General of the Colony. In 1690, William Byrd built a wooden dwelling which later was burned. His son, Colonel William Byrd, the second, founder of the city of Richmond, inherited the plantation. About 1730, he built the present brick house. William Byrd, the third of the name, and son of the second, became proprietor of Westover in his turn and left the property at his death to his wife, Mary, daughter of Anne Shippen and Charles Willing of Philadelphia. Upon her death, in 1814, Westover passed from the Byrd family. The property has changed hands often since then. From Colonel John Selden, who planted the row of tulip poplars on the river side of the house, Westover passed to Major Augustus Drewry. Mrs. Clarice Sears Ramsay, who laid out the present garden, rebuilt the two-story east wing, and river wall, was the next in line to occupy the estate. The present owner, Mrs. Richard Crane, and the late Mr. Crane, succeeded in adding great charm and in restoring southern hospitality and ancient glory to the old place.

The gracious site, close to the river, has a thousand associations. Tradition has it that Evelyn Byrd, daughter of the second William Byrd, and reigning belle of the colony, pined away and died of a broken heart through love of Earl Peterborough, whom her father rejected as a suitor.

During the War of Independence, the British forces, under Benedict Arnold, landed at Westover on their way to Richmond and again on their return from the Capital. Prior to the seige of Yorktown, Lord Cornwallis camped and crossed the James river at this point. In 1862, the residence was ransacked, partly burned and greatly damaged while within the entrenched camp of Harrison's Landing.

One scarcely knows which part of Westover is most to be admired—whether it be the site, the trees, the old wrought-iron gates, or the glorious house—which often has been acclaimed "the most perfect Georgian architecture in America." When one has wandered over the lawn, has viewed the building from all angles, and has examined the mysterious tunnel that leads to the river, one must go to the beautiful garden, where under a quaint tombstone William Byrd, "the black Swan" lies buried. The inscription on his memorial is as follows:

"Here lyeth

The Honorable William Byrd, Esqr.

"Being born to one of the amplest fortunes in this country, he was sent early to England for his education, where, under the care and direction of Sir Robert Southwell, and even with his particular instructions, he made a happy proficiency in polite and various learning; by the means of the same noble friend he was introduced to the acquaintance of many of the first persons of that age for knowledge, wit, virtue, birth, or high station, and particularly attracted a most close and bosom friendship with the learned and illustrious Charles Boyle, Earl of Orrery.

"He was admitted to the bar in the Middle Temple, studied for some time in the low countries, visited the court of France, and was chosen fellow of the Royal Society.

"Thus eminently fitted for the service and ornament of his country, he was made receiver-general of his Majesty's revenues here, was thrice appointed publick agent to the court and ministry of

England; and being thirty seven years a member, at last became president of the Council of this Colony. To all this were added a great elegancy of taste and life, the well-bred gentleman and polite companion, the splendid economist and prudent father of a family, with the constant enemy of all exhorbitant power and hearty friend to the liberties of his country. Nat. March 28, 1674. Mort. Aug. 26, 1744. Aetat 70."

WESTOVER CHURCH

Old Indian Trail · Route 5, Charles City County

BACK ON THE highroad and crossing the bridge over Herring Creek, one is on the way to Westover Church. This ancient Parish was established before 1652, with its original church on the southern slope to the river, on the present Westover estate. There, amid peace and quiet, may still be seen the tombs of Mary Byrd, wife of one and mother of another of the distinguished William Byrds and of Evelyn Byrd, the fair heroine of romance. Among the other old graves are those of the Harrisons and Burwell families.

The present church is said to have been "removed brick by brick by Mrs. Byrd to her land 'Evelyngton' about two miles away," between 1737 and 1748, during the rectorate of the Reverend Peter Fontaine, son of a Huguenot refugee. Tradition says the reason for the change of site was that virtually the whole congregation remained after services for mid-day dinner at Westover. Even Virginia hospitality could not endure that endlessly.

The last interment in the old churchyard was that of Evelyn Byrd in 1737. The earliest unbroken tombstone in the "new" churchyard is one "Erected by Richard Weir, To the dear memory of his pupil and friend—June 17, 1748."

The church itself later suffered greatly because of the military operations that centered about it during two wars. British troopers are said to have used the sacred structure as a stable for their mounts. Sixty-one years afterwards the church was within the line of defences, many parts of which still remain, that General McClellan erected on Evelyngton Heights to cover the entrenched camp at Harrison's Landing. Not far from the site of the church, July 3, 1862, General J. E. B. Stuart incautiously fired into the Federal camps with the only howitzer attached to his cavalry. This gave the alarm to the Unionists who otherwise might have left the Heights unguarded. All these events now seem remote in distance as in time from the quiet house of prayer, which has been restored with care and is used regularly for service.

RIVER EDGE

Old Indian Trail · *Route 5, Charles City County*

BETWEEN Westover Church and River Edge, the road winds for three and a half miles up and down hills, through patches of slender pine and by far reaching well cultivated fields. Two miles east of Westover Church, one passes on the left Indian Fields, while just west of River Edge entrance is Cloverfields. River Edge was originally composed of ten thousand acres of land along the James River from Gunn's Run to Herring Creek. This tract was a grant from the crown to William Cole, Esquire, of Bothrope, Warwick County, sometime member of the Virginia Council, Secretary of State and one of the first trustees of the College of William and Mary. His son, William Cole, the second, a member of the House of Burgesses for Warwick County and Deputy, Receiver-General and Colonel of Militia, inherited the estate. As early as 1714, there were warehouses on the property, and it is thought that the house was built at this time, but there are no records to prove the date. At a later time, likewise unestablished, the original dwelling was moved from the river to the present site. In 1769, William Cole, the fourth to bear the name, sold four thousand acres of his plantation to William Byrd of Westover. After the sale he moved to Albemarle County, Virginia. Sixty odd years later, the little story and a half dwelling with many less acres was the residence of Doctor Edward Wilcox, whose family and descendants occupied it for many years. After the War Between the States, River Edge changed ownership many times until 1925, when the property was bought and restored to its former charm and usefulness by Mr. and Mrs. Lamar Curry Thomas. The once informal ivy covered dwelling is now the beautifully remodelled and greatly enlarged residence of Mr. and Mrs. Sam Anthony Mason.

The chief historical associations of River Edge are with the historic preliminaries of the dramatic "crossing of the James" by the army of the Potomac, June 14-17, 1864. Virtually the whole Federal host passed over the estate enroute to Wilcox Wharf. Thence it was transported over the river to "Windmill Point" where for the long operations in front of Petersburg Sir George Yeardley built the first windmill in America.

GREENWAY

Old Indian Trail · Route 5, Charles City County

MORE CURVING wooded road, over Gunn's Run Bridge, up the hill, and in the distance on the left hand side of the road is Greenway. This quaint old story and a half clapboard house stands back from the road in what was once an avenue of tall and graceful locust trees, alas no more. Here was the home of Governor John Tyler, of Williamsburg, who moved to Charles City County just before the Revolutionary War and married Mary Armistead. Their son John Tyler, later to become Governor of Virginia and tenth President of the United States, was born here in the spring of 1790. To this circumstance and to the birth of William Henry Harrison at Berkeley, Charles City County owes the distinction of being the cradle of two Presidents. Westmoreland County, Virginia, gave birth to Washington and to Monroe; the Adamses, father and son, were born at Braintree, Massachusetts, before Braintree and Quincy were separated; but Charles City is unique in having given America a President who died in office, and the Vice-President who succeeded him.

Greenway has changed hands countless times and is now owned by the Beal brothers.

CHARLES CITY COURT HOUSE

Old Indian Trail · Route 5, Charles City County

WITHIN SIGHT of Greenway are the stout old walls of Charles City Court House, reared about 1710, which witnessed much of the violence that has swept the Peninsula of Virginia.

During the War of Independence, Lieutenant-Colonel Simcoe and a detachment of the Queen's Rangers made a surprise attack here, killed one, wounded three and took several prisoners. In 1862-65, the Court House stood for many months close to the grim borders of No-Man's Land and suffered accordingly. The building was ransacked, its valuable records were looted, some destroyed, others thrown in the fields, and still others carried to the North. In the last few years, a number of these missing records have been returned. Despite this ill fortune, the Court House in the shade of its old trees remains substantially unchanged. It could be identified easily today from extant photographs of 1862.

The monument in the courtyard was erected to the soldiers in the War Between the States and bears the following inscription:

"To the Confederate Soldiers of Charles City County

1861-1865

Defenders of Constitutional Liberty and the Rights of Self-Government.

Erected A. D. 1900

Pro Aris Et Focis."

BUSH HILL

Old Indian Trail · Route 5, Charles City County

AT THE FOOT of the hill one keeps to the right over Court House Creek and in less than a half a mile to the left is a sign marked Bush Hill. On a slight incline in a noble old grove, among which are two ancient paradise trees, stands an interesting two and a half story dwelling. Unlike the other houses visited this is a tall square building with full basement and two rooms on each floor. The front entrance is through a very wide door facing south which opens into a square hall whose plain pine stairs ascend to the third floor. On the east is the beautifully proportioned dining room whose paneled mantel with its concealed shelves is said to have influenced the design of the one in the Raleigh Tavern in Williamsburg. Down one step from the dining room is a story and a half later addition. The only entrance to the room above is by way of steep steps concealed in a closet in the down stairs room. In the yard are the Doctor's old office, smoke house and slave quarters.

The date of the erection of this residence is unknown, the county records having been destroyed, but the deed of 1811 refers to the property as "being a part of the tract of land formerly belonging to William Greene Munford." He was the second of that name and the son of William Greene Munford, Justice of Charles City County from 1769 to 1781, Major of Charles City Militia and a member of the House of Delegates. In the will of William Munford, the elder, dated February 8, 1786, he leaves his lands to his four sons.

Among other prominent persons who owned the property were Cary Wilkinson, a physician who served on the Committee for James City County in 1774, Doctors James B. Mc. Caw, Edmund O. Christian and Junius Roan. During Doctor Roan's residence, in the spring of 1864, the Federal troops made a surprise attack on a number of Confederate soldiers encamped on Bush Hill wounding several and making prisoners of almost the entire command.

Since the early part of the twentieth century, the place has remained in the Waddill family. It is now owned and occupied by Mrs. Louise Waddill Mc. Intyre who is carefully restoring it.

WEYANOKE

Old Indian Trail · Route 5, Charles City County

ONE MILE EAST of Bush Hill, at the fork of the road, a sign reads "Weyanoke." To visit the Weyanokes necessitates a round trip drive of nine and a half miles over dirt roads, but, if one loves old houses with far-reaching views of the circling James, they will not be disappointed. We shall first visit lower Weyanoke, the most distant in years and miles.

Long before the white man came to these shores, a tribe of Indians under the governorship of the "Queen of the Weyanokes" had their seat here. In 1617, Opechancanough, brother of Powhatan, bestowed twenty-two hundred acres of land upon Sir George Yeardley, Governor of the Colony, but it was not until two years thereafter that the gift was confirmed by the London Company. In 1624, or thereabout, Captain Abraham Peirsey purchased the property from Governor Yeardley. Twenty odd years elapsed before Joseph Harwood obtained Weyanoke, which remained in the possession of his descendants for generations. It was William Harwood who, in 1740, erected the center part of the present large two-story frame dwelling.

Before the War Between the States, the garden of Weyanoke was considered one of the loveliest in Virginia. Alas, after the Cold Harbor defeat, a remnant of Sheridan's army marched through it.

Today, after various transfers, the beautifully remodelled residence and well kept plantation is the summer home of the Lawrence Lewises.

UPPER WEYANOKE

Old Indian Trail · Route 5, Charles City County

ONE RETRACES the journey one mile to the sign on the left hand side of the road and makes a very sharp left turn into Upper Weyanoke.

A few years prior to the War Between the States, Mary Willis Marshall, granddaughter of the Chief Justice, came to live at Upper Weyanoke as the beautiful young bride of Fielding Lewis Douthat.

As previously stated, this lovely old plantation on the edges of the winding James was a part of the original grant to Sir George Yeardley. The ancient mansion has long since disappeared and there remains only the sturdy little story and a half brick dwelling, the scene of "To Have and to Hold," now attractively restored and used as a summer cottage by Dr. and Mrs. Alexander Yelverton Peyton Garnett, the owners of the estate. In the much later spacious red brick residence reside the gracious descendants of the lovely Mary Willis Marshall. Here, too, is her sweet, old-fashion garden tended by loving hands.

SHERWOOD FOREST

Old Indian Trail · Route 5, Charles City County

A FRACTION over a half a mile from the Weyanokes' highroad sign, on the right is Burlington, one time home of Judge John M. Gregory, the acting Governor of Virginia in 1842. Less than a mile and a half farther, at the turn in the road, behind an old whitewashed fence in an ancient grove of trees, is the long two and a half story, yellow clapboard house, with its many additions of varying height, dubbed the longest house in America.

Sherwood Forest, originally Walnut Grove, the home of the Minge family, was sold in 1842 to John Tyler, who was residing here when he was notified of the death of President William Henry Harrison. At the expiration of his term as successor to Harrison, John Tyler retired to this estate with his second wife, nee Julia Gardiner. Rejected by the Whig party for his adherence to his political principles, Tyler facetiously likened himself to the "outlaw" Robin Hood and changed the name of Walnut Grove to Sherwood Forest.

After McClellan's retreat from Harrison's Landing, part of the army rested here on its way to Yorktown, whence it was to embark for Northern Virginia. Two years later when Sheridan and his officers encamped here, the house was occupied by soldiers, the household furniture was wrecked and all movables were carted off. Fortunately, many of the papers of the vast Tyler collection of historical manuscripts were left on the floors of the rooms and later were reclaimed.

At the death of President Tyler in January, 1862, his estate passed to his oldest son, by his second wife, the late Judge D. Gardiner Tyler, whose descendants Mr. and Mrs. Alfred G. Tyler still occupy the residence.

One continues on Old Indian Trail through beautiful stretches of woodland, by countless by-roads to ancient dwellings which due to their inaccessibility and their sad state of dilapidation are not visited. Before crossing the Chickahominy River at Barret's Forge to James City County, one passes the inviting entrace to Tomahund, one time residence of the Morecock and Lightfoot families.

133

JAMES CITY COUNTY, VIRGINIA

JAMES CITY COUNTY, the most historic one of the eight original shires divided in 1634, was named for Jamestown or James City. At this point the Peninsula is so narrow that in colonial times the county enjoyed the luxury of deep water. Skirting its northern boundary is the York River and on its southern border flows the James.

Within its hundred and eighty odd square miles was born the American Nation. In 1607, the first permanent English settlement on this continent was established at Jamestown. The early stockade was christened in honor of King James, the first, of England. Through its dismal swamps and virgin forests crept the savage Indian. Distrust and misunderstanding between the Indian and the White Man caused bloodshed and massacres. "Down times' lengthening way" increased the unrest and fear of the pioneer. The tyrannical rule of the Royal Governors finally led, in 1676, to Bacon's Rebellion. This uprising lit the spark which smouldered a hundred years before bursting into flame in the War of American Independence.

The British army under Cornwallis, having broken camp at Williamsburg, arrived in this vicinity July 4, 1781, en route to Jamestown Island, where Cornwallis planned to cross the James River and march to Portsmouth. About one mile and a half from Greenspring on the Williamsburg road, Lafayette's troops made an unsuccessful attack on the Britishers. Cornwallis made no attempt to pursue but under cover of darkness crossed the James River and proceeded to Portsmouth.

James City was again the scene of camp fires and fierce fighting during the four tragic years of the War Between the States. After the retreat from Yorktown in May, 1862, until the close of the war in April, 1865, Williamsburg, which is situated on the dividing line of James City and York Counties, was within the Federal lines.

James City County boasts of having within its boundaries the second Capital of the Old Dominion and the second oldest college in the United States.

134

WILLIAMSBURG

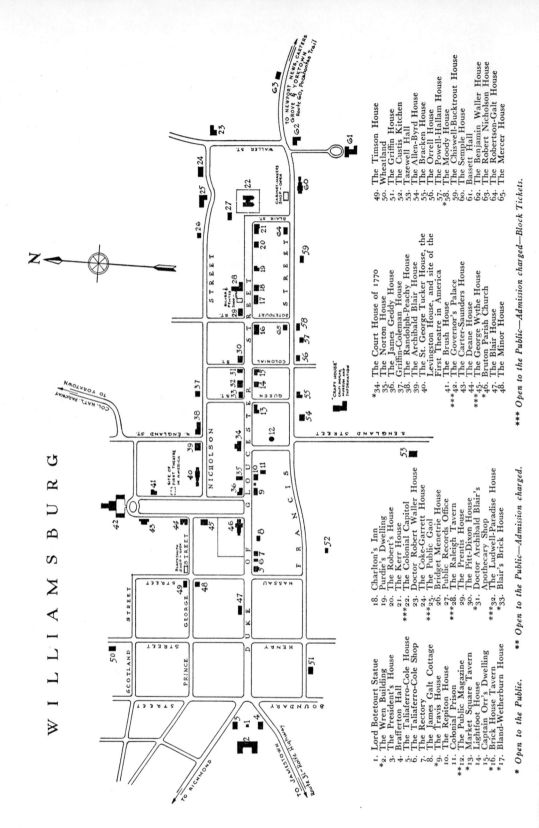

WILLIAMSBURG

 1. Lord Botetourt Statue
*2. The Wren Building
*3. The President's House
 4. Brafferton Hall
 5. The Taliaferro-Cole House
 6. The Taliaferro-Cole Shop
 7. The Rectory
 8. The James Galt Cottage
*9. The Travis House
10. The Repiton House
11. Colonial Prison
**12. The Public Magazine
13. Market Square Tavern
15. Captain Orr's Dwelling
*16. Brick House Tavern
17. Bland-Wetherburn House

18. Charlton's Inn
19. Purdie's Dwelling
20. The Robert's House
21. The Kerr House
***22. The Colonial Capitol
23. Doctor Robert Waller House
24. The Coke-Garrett House
***25. The Public Gaol
26. Bridget Menetrie House
27. Public Records Office
***28. The Raleigh Tavern
29. The Prentis House
30. The Pitt-Dixon House
31. Doctor Archibald Blair's Apothecary Shop
***32. The Ludwell-Paradise House
33. Blair's Brick House

*34. The Court House of 1770
35. The Norton House
36. The James Geddy House
37. Griffin-Coleman House
38. The Randolph-Peachy House
39. The Archibald Blair House
40. The St. George Tucker House, the Levingston House, and site of the First Theatre in America
*41. The Brush House
****42. The Governor's Palace
43. The Carter-Saunders House
44. The Deane House
****45. The George Wythe House
*46. Bruton Parish Church
47. The Blair House
48. The Minor House

49. The Timson House
50. Wheatland
51. The Griffin House
52. The Custis Kitchen
53. Tazewell Hall
54. The Allen-Byrd House
55. The Bracken House
56. The Orrell House
57. The Powell-Hallam House
*58. The Moody House
59. The Chiswell-Bucktrout House
60. The Semple House
61. Bassett Hall
62. The Benjamin Waller House
63. The Robert Nicholson House
64. The Robertson-Galt House
65. The Mercer House

* Open to the Public.   ** Open to the Public—Admission charged.   *** Open to the Public—Admission charged—Block Tickets.

WILLIAMSBURG

HAVING CROSSED the lovely new bridge at Barret's Ferry over the Chickahominy River, one is a little over ten miles from Williamsburg. The traveler, on entering the old Colonial Capital, is at once conscious of the determined and successful effort to subordinate modern business to the calm beauty of the eighteenth century. History is turned back. One walks streets and enters great houses where the illusion is so complete that one expects a periwigged gentleman to step out of the next door, or a lady in a sedan chair to turn the next corner. No city in America is quite like Williamsburg. To none should the visitor come with a purpose firmer to forget speed and haste and to live serenely to slow time.

Doctor John Pott, President of the Council, Governor of the Colony and "esteemed the best surgeon and physician" of his day in Virginia, patented on the present site of Williamsburg twelve hundred acres of land, June 6, 1632. This property he styled "Middle Plantation" because it was on the watershed midway between the York and the James. Sixty years elapsed before Theodorick Bland surveyed the land and laid it out in lots for the town of Williamsburg, patriotically so named in honor of William, the third. In 1699, the town became the capital of the colony and, in 1722, an incorporated city, the first in Virginia. The next seventy-five years were the golden age of Williamsburg. There at intervals met the General Assembly of Virginia, the oldest representative body of lawmakers in the Anglo-Saxon New World. Thither, from their plantations, came the members of the Council, their wives and their families. Litigants thronged the inns. Pleasure-goers sought out the theatres. A press and, for a time, three newspapers spread to the frontier the glories of the little town. Those Virginia youths who were not sent to England for study attended the College of William and Mary. Until the eve of the Revolution, Williamsburg was the gayest and probably the most cultured city in the Southern colonies. Virtually all the relics that have survived that era show a society that was graceful and well-furnished.

When the Revolution began, Williamsburg was much exposed to raids from the rivers. The Burgesses could not meet there in safety. They adjourned to Richmond and, in 1779, made that city their capital. The splendor of Williamsburg faded fast. Plundering and arson during the campaign of 1781 were followed by neglect and decay. Brave old families kept their homes and their customs. Industry and government moved to the head of navigation. The sceptre of power passed to Midland Virginia. The College of William and Mary, long without a rival in Virginia, found its clientele divided with Hampden-Sidney and with the University of Virginia, even before the rise of denominational colleges in the fourth decade of the eighteenth century.

What was left of beauty was marred still more during the War Between the States. After the retreat from Yorktown, May 3, 1862, General Joseph E. Johnston fought a rearguard action at Williamsburg, May 4-5, and then in hasty retreat to protect his rear, had to move westward and had even to leave his wounded to the care of a grieving but loyal population. From that time until the close of the war, except for one or two hasty raids, Williamsburg was within the Federal lines, garrisoned and slowly dismembered. Nothing but the loyal efforts of the women and the old men saved the town from ruin.

Recovery was slow and uncertain. There was no railroad to link the city with Richmond and with Yorktown until the hundredth anniversary of Yorktown. River travel was at the end of roads sand-bound in summer and bottomless with mud in winter. The College rehabilitated itself with an effort, but of industry there was little. Not a few of the exquisite old homes that had survived war and disrepair were maintained through the efforts of loyal sons and daughters of the city who went inland or Northward and there earned money they gladly spent to save the ancestral walls and roof.

Still a third time war touched Williamsburg, and in a manner different far from that of 1781 or of 1862. Soon after the United States were forced to hostilities in 1917, a great shell-loading plant was constructed on York River. A mushroom town know as Penniman was built. Williamsburg was the nearest city to this aggregation of factories and dormitories. A friendly foe, the workers in this munitions plant, "took" Williamsburg. Amusement houses and restaurants sprang up. Strange music echoed through quiet streets. Every spare room was in demand. Business expanded without regard to the loveliness of the old town. More surely than at any time in its history, Williamsburg was in danger of change so swift and so unthinking as to threaten the death of all that had made the town graciously beautiful.

When conditions were at their worst, the Reverend W. A. R. Goodwin returned to the rectorate of Bruton Church. He had served that parish during the years when the tercentenary of the founding of Virginia was being observed, and he then had restored the old church with admirable taste and small means. Upon his acceptance of a second rectorate, he saw with startled eyes the demolition that had been wrought in the name of progress and he realized that what he had done for Bruton must be done for the older section of the entire city. Otherwise Williamsburg would be architecturally beyond redemption. At first, as he talked of a general restoration, skeptics thought him a dreamer. Millions of dollars would be required to restore Williamsburg. Whence would the money come? Doctor Goodwin's answer was that funds could and would be found. At length, in 1927, he interested John D. Rockefeller, Jr. That great philanthropist determined to undertake the restoration, but with rare vision insisted that if it were done at all, it had to be done perfectly. The restoration of a shell of the town —a few facades on a main street, behind which twentieth-century life was lived in his bustle and jazz—did not interest him. Ere he had finished, he had utilized some of the best abilities of America in architecture, in landscape design, in historical research and in decoration, and he had spent unostentatiously some fifteen million dollars, but the work was as perfect as he had demanded. A dozen properties, perhaps, remain to be acquired in the restoration area. The others, with incredible skill and patience, have been made once more a lovely eighteenth-century town.

The restoration centers about Duke of Gloucester Street, which one enters by the Rolfe Highway (Route 31). It is convenient to stop first at the Information Bureau in the Craft House, on the right hand side of the Williamsburg Inn on Francis Street. The itinerary observed on the pages that follow begins at the college and goes eastward through the city. All residences are privately occupied and are not open to the public.

LORD BOTETOURT STATUE

The College of William and Mary in Virginia

West End of Duke of Gloucester Street · No. 1 on Williamsburg map

IF ONE ENTERS the campus of William and Mary College in the early morning with the dew sparkling on each blade of grass and the sun peeping through the leaves of noble old trees, the desire will be to remain many hours. In the center of the brick pathway leading to the Wren building, pause and view the interesting old marble statue of Lord Botetourt. Its inscription tells the story:

LORD BOTETOURT STATUE
By
Richard Hayward
of London
1773
Erected by an appropriation
of the General Assembly

LORD BOTETOURT
Born 1718—Died 1770
Norborne Berkeley
Baron de Botetourt
Governor-in-Chief
October 28, 1768 to October 15, 1770.

"The Right Honorable Norborne Berkeley, Baron de Botetourt, his Majesty's late Lieutenant; and Governor-General of the Colony and Dominion of Virginia.

"Deeply impressed with the warmest sense of gratitude for his Excellency's, the Right Honorable Lord Botetourt's, prudent and wise administration, and that the remembrance of those many public and social virtues which so eminently adorned his illustrious character might be transmitted to posterity, the General Assembly of Virginia, on the xx day of July, Ann. Dom., MDCCLXXI resolved with one united voice to erect this statue to his Lordship's memory. Let wisdom and justice preside in any country, the people must and will be happy.

"America, behold your friend, who leaving his native country declined those additional honors which were there in store for him, that he might heal your wounds and restore tranquillity and happiness to this extensive continent. With what zeal and anxiety he pursued these glorious objects, Virginia thus bears her grateful testimony."

THE WREN BUILDING

The College of William and Mary in Virginia

West End of Duke of Gloucester Street · No. 2 on Williamsburg map

MOUNTING THE broad steps of the Wren Building, one enters through the massive doors into the second oldest college in the United States. This historic original building is a monument to many men. Among them, Francis Nicholson, Governor of Virginia, and James Blair, a native of Edinburgh, Scotland and rector of Varina Parish, in Henrico County, and of Bruton Parish, in James City County, were enthusiastic workers in behalf of establishing a free school and college in Virginia. Blair, who was sent to England in 1691 to raise the necessary money and to obtain a charter, secured the support of King William and Queen Mary. Two years later he returned with a charter, dated February 8, 1693, and with a generous endowment. After various locations had been considered, three hundred and fifty acres of land at "Middle Plantation" were purchased as the site of the new college, which was named William and Mary College, in honor of their Majesties. Under the supervision of Thomas Hadley, an English architect, plans attributed to Sir Christopher Wren were put in execution. In 1697, the building was partially completed. By 1700, when students were living in it, classes were being held under James Blair, the first President, and Mungo Ingles, a Scotchman, the grammar master. Twenty years later, the original chapel in the southern wing was begun under the direction of Henry Cary. On June 28, 1732, it was opened with religious ceremonies conducted by the President. In the crypt of the chapel are five vaults and one grave. These are the resting places of Sir John Randolph, Lord Botetourt, Peyton Randolph and his wife Betty, John Randolph, Attorney-General, Bishop James Madison and his wife, Chancellor Thomas Nelson and an unknown student.

The corresponding northern wing of the Wren Building was used as a library but was destroyed in the fire of 1859. Until the completion of the Capitol in Williamsburg, the courts of the colony and the General Assembly held their meetings and had their offices in the Wren building. Here, also, the Colonial Clergy had their conventions.

During the Revolutionary war the College was used as a hospital. Numbers of troops died here from wounds received at Yorktown. The coming of the War Between the States soon placed the College immediately in rear of General J. B. Magruder's Confederate lines at Yorktown and on Warwick River. After the battle of Williamsburg, May 4-5, 1862, the College was occupied by Federal troops, the library was looted, and the building partially burned. On the return of peace to the ravaged Peninsula, reconstruction of the college was slow. For several years, its dauntless old President, Colonel Benjamin Stoddert Ewell, could do no more than ring the bell on the opening day, enroll one student to keep the charter alive, and then close the college to await better days. Largely through the efforts of President Lyon G. Tyler it received an annual State appropriation, which has been increased and has been supplemented by other funds until today the college, which has been coeducational since 1918, has more than thirteen hundred students. The President of the college is John Stewart Bryan.

Through the generosity of John D. Rockefeller, Jr., the original building has been restored and greatly beautified. On its walls is a tablet that commemorates the College's many priorities in education, another to bear witness to the continuity of this building through centuries of service, and still another to the Phi Beta Kappa Society, progenitor and model of all college fraternities, which was founded at Raleigh Tavern by students of William and Mary in 1776. The wording of the priorities tablet is as follows:

PRIORITIES

OF THE COLLEGE OF WILLIAM AND MARY.

Chartered February 8, 1693, by King William and Queen Mary.
Main building designed by Sir Christopher Wren.

FIRST College in the United States in its antecedents, which go back to the College proposed at Henrico (1619). Second to Harvard University in actual operation.

144

First American College to receive its charter from the Crown under the Seal of the Privy Council, 1693. Hence it was known as "their Majesties' Royal College of William and Mary."

First and ONLY American College to receive a Coat-of-Arms from the College of Heralds, 1694.

First College in the United States to have a full Faculty, consisting of a President, six Professors, usher, and writing master, 1729.

First College to confer medallic prizes: the gold medals donated by Lord Botetourt in 1771.

First College to establish an inter-collegiate fraternity, the Phi Beta Kappa, December 5, 1776.

First College to have the Elective System of study, 1779.

First College to have the Honor System, 1779.

First College to become a University, 1779.

First College to have a school of Modern Languages, 1779.

First College to have a school of Municipal and Constitutional Law, 1779.

First College to teach Political Economy, 1784.

First College to have a school of Modern History, 1803.

Presented by the Colonial Capital Branch of
The Association for the
Preservation of Virginia Antiquities,
1914.

THE PRESIDENT'S HOUSE

The College of William and Mary in Virginia

West End of Duke of Gloucester Street · No. 3 on Williamsburg map

THE PRESIDENT'S HOUSE on the campus of William and Mary, adjoining the Pocahontas Trail to Richmond, dates from 1732. It is renowned architecturally for the angle of its roof, but it is in all other respects a notable Georgian structure and it has fascinating historical association. During the War of Independence, Lord Cornwallis temporarily had his headquarters here. Upon the arrival of the French troops, it was used by them as a military hospital. While so occupied, it was accidentally burned and later was restored with funds from the privy purse of Louis the Fourteenth. Like the nearby college, the President's house suffered again during the War Between the States, but it has been restored flawlessly. A defacing porch that long fronted the campus has been removed. This has brought back in just proportion the fine lines of the structure. It is believed that everyone of the twenty Presidents of the college, from Reverend James Blair to Doctor John Stewart Bryan, has lived here for at least part of his term of office.

BRAFFERTON HALL

The College of William and Mary in Virginia

West End of Duke of Gloucester Street · No. 4 on Williamsburg map

As Brafferton Hall, opposite the President's House, has the date 1723 carved in a brick near the door, this is thought to record the year of its erection. It was built through the interest of the Earl of Burlington, nephew of Honorable Robert Boyle and executor of his uncle's will. The will provided that £4000 be devoted to "pious and charitable uses." This money was invested in Brafferton Manor, Yorkshire, England, the rents of which were to be the revenue for the Indian School. The Reverend James Blair, while in England, obtained the yield from this fund, which was paid the college until the Revolutionary War. After the stoppage of the fund, the Indian School ceased to exist. Along with the other College buildings, Brafferton was used in 1862-65 by Federal troops, who carried away all the fine old woodwork. Subsequently, Brafferton served as the administration offices of William and Mary. In recent years the building has been restored with fine regard for its noble lines.

THE TALIAFERRO-COLE HOUSE
AND THE TALIAFERRO-COLE SHOP

Duke of Gloucester and Nassau Streets · Nos. 5 and 6 on Williamsburg map

THE HURRIED VISITOR may leave the beautiful campus by the front entrance and may begin inspection of Duke of Gloucester Street. On both sides of the first square are attractive new buildings in ancient garb. On the left is the charming one-story, red-brick bank with hipped roof and cupola. A few doors east, set back in a sort of a court, is the whitewashed U. S. Post Office. In the nineteenth century, on the west corner on the right hand side of the next block stood a large wooden dwelling occupied by the eccentric, but beloved Baptist preacher, the Reverend Scervant Jones, who held his religious meetings in the Powder Magazine. On the adjoining lots, in 1734, stood the residence and office of William Blaikley, whose wife, Catherine, became one of the best known midwives of the colony.

On the south east corner is the square shaped full two-story clapboard dwelling built sometime prior to 1752, by Charles Taliaferro, a coach and chair maker. By 1803, the property had passed to Jesse Cole, later Postmaster of Williamsburg under President Andrew Jackson.

Adjoining its old-fashion garden is a reconstructed one-story building long called the "Pulaski Club." In a letter of 1827, De La Pena, professor of French at William and Mary College, referred to a building then used as the Post Office, in the center of the Main Street, as the curiosity of the town. He described it as "A book-seller's store in which you will find hams and French brandy; it is an apothecary's shop in which you can provide yourself with black silk stockings and shell oysters; it is a post office in which you may have glisters and chewing tobacco and in a word it is a museum of natural history, in which we meet every afternoon to dispute about the presidential election and the quality of irish potatoes." This small building justifies its claim to be the oldest store in Williamsburg. It and the residence were inherited by Jesse Cole's grandson, Henry Denison Cole who occupied them until his death several years ago.

THE RECTORY

NEXT DOOR to the Taliaferro-Cole Shop is the white clapboard dwelling known as the Rectory. It is a full two-story, square building, with five dormer windows across its gable roof. The basement is half above the ground and the main entrance is through a small pillared portico.

Shortly before the War Between the States, the house was erected for the Reverend John T. James. After serving as the Rectory for Bruton Parish for many years, it was purchased by the Restoration, and in 1928 and 1929, the house was modernized for the use of the officials of the Colonial Williamsburg, Incorporated.

THE JAMES GALT COTTAGE

Duke of Gloucester Street · No. 8 on Williamsburg map

AFTER LEAVING the Rectory and passing the small restored Maupin shop, one stands in front of a picket fence enclosing the quaint little story and a half, clapboard house and inviting boxwood garden, which was originally on the Eastern State Hospital grounds. This little dwelling was the home of James Galt, surgeon in the Revolutionary War and keeper of the hospital. Fifty odd years later, his son, William Trebell Galt, then superintendent of the hospital as well as the Mayor of Williamsburg, occupied the residence. After the fire in the summer of 1885, which destroyed the hospital, the Galt Cottage alone remained without damage. In the course of the Williamsburg Restoration, the dwelling was moved from the hospital grounds and was rebuilt on Duke of Gloucester Street where it now stands.

THE TRAVIS HOUSE

Duke of Gloucester Street · No. 9 on Williamsburg map

SEPARATING the James Galt Cottage and the Travis House is the John Custis Tenement and garden, referred to as "Maupin-Dixon House" by its occupants. The Travis House, which was originally on Francis Street, is a long, one room deep, story and a half, clapboard building, with Dutch roof and dormer windows. One enters from the street by a few steps into a small, square hall through which is a glimpse of a charming old garden.

The dwelling was built in 1765 by Edward Champion Travis, a prominent gentleman of his day. He was a member of the House of Burgesses from Jamestown and owned virtually the entire island. At the beginning of the Revolution his son, Colonel Champion Travis, was a Burgess from Jamestown and subsequently, served on the Court of Directors of the Eastern State Hospital.

The Colonel's son, Samuel, fought in the War of 1812. His son-in-law, the famous agriculturist, Edmund Ruffin, of "Shellbanks," Coggins Point, Prince George County, is said by some authorities to have fired at Fort Sumter, Charleston, South Carolina, the shot that opened the War Between the States.

For many years, the Travis dwelling was used as a residence for the superintendent of the Eastern State Hospital. As a part of the Restoration, it was moved to its present site on Duke of Gloucester Street and was given new glory. Still called "The Travis House," it serves many hungry visitors to Williamsburg in 18th century style.

THE REPITON HOUSE

Duke of Gloucester Street · No. 10 on Williamsburg map

NEXT DOOR to the Travis House and adjoining the Colonial Prison in the rear is a charming little story and a half frame dwelling and office. The history of this site is vague, but from the scraps found, it is most interesting. The property was owned by the corporation of the City of Williamsburg and leased to private citizens. This point on Duke of Gloucester Street is the dividing line of the counties, here James City County begins. During the eighteenth century the house was on a corner, as originally the bounds of Market Square ran just east of it. There is no authentic date of its erection, but the City of Williamsburg was leasing the corporation lands in 1745.

The first recorded owner is John Greenhow, who resided in a house on the site of the Travis House, where he also had a large shop. This property he rented. In its early existence it was a boot shop conducted by George Wilson, a master shoemaker who imported his materials from England. In 1806, Louis Hue Girardin, then professor of Modern Language at the College of William and Mary, purchased the wooden dwelling from John Greenhow. By 1815, Joseph Repiton had acquired it and the old brick prison. In 1828, Repiton sold the entire property to David Mason. After years of litigation, the following advertisement appeared in the Phoenix-Gazette:

1857

"To be sold! one half of the house and lot now occupied by Mrs. Elizabeth D. Mason situated on the south side of Main Street in the City of Williamsburg and bounded on the East by Market Square. The house is divided into two sectional halves by the passage and stairway, which are common to both sections, and the half to be sold is the left section as you approach the dwelling from Main Street, consisting of two good rooms on the lower floor and one on the upper, cellar and office attached—." The next issue of the paper said "the passage and staircase was not to be used by the purchaser of the above half, neither can the lot and well be used in common."

At one time the house was used for the Post Office, later as a bakery and finally razed to make way for the bank.

COLONIAL PRISON

James City County-Williamsburg Jail

Market Square · No. 11 on Williamsburg map

LEAVING the Repiton dwelling, with its interesting tiny white office and quaint out-buildings, one sees in its rear, facing Market Square, the Colonial Prison. The small, brick, one-story, gable roof prison, with its huge outside chimney, is owned and occupied by the Daughters of the American Revolution as their headquarters.

After the removal of the capitol from Jamestown, the county court continued to be held there until 1706. Then it, too, was transferred to Williamsburg. Thriftily, the House of Burgesses provided that the bricks of the old State House at Jamestown should be used for the building of a new court house in the second capitol. This was done about 1716. Approximately at the same time, a county prison was erected for the imprisonment of petty criminals, the custody of runaway apprentices and slaves and the detention of prisoners awaiting trial before the General Court. Debtors were under the jurisdiction of the General Court and were confined in a special wing of the public gaol on Nicholson Street.

In 1770, when the new joint Williamsburg-James City County Court House was completed, James City County Court House and prison were sold to private persons. For a time the prison was used as a lumber house, but later was occupied as a dwelling.

THE PUBLIC MAGAZINE

Market Square · No. 12 on Williamsburg map

FACING THE Colonial Prison in the center of Market Square and England Street is the Powder Magazine.

This unique structure, which was both metaphorically and literally a Powder Magazine, was built in 1714, during Alexander Spotswood's Governorship. At the beginning of the War of Independence, by order of Lord Dunmore, the powder stored there was transferred by Captain Henry Collins and some sailors to a man-of-war under Captain Montague. This seizure of powder owned by the colonists proved great excitement and indignation. Revolutionaries started a march on Williamsburg. Colonel Carter Braxton of "Elsing Green," on the Pamunkey River, acted for the colonists in demanding either the return of the explosive or payment for it in full. After parleys, he received a bill of exchange for £320. This he delivered to Captain Patrick Henry, who was encamped at Doncastle's Ordinary in New Kent County.

After the Revolutionary War, the old Powder Magazine was used for various purposes. First it was a market and then a Baptist meeting house under the leadership of Elder Scervant Jones. On week days it was a dancing school. In its ultimate disrepair, it degenerated into a stable. Finally, it was bought by the Association for the Preservation of Virginia Antiquities, in whose possession it remains as a museum and is open to the public. It has been restored by Colonial Williamsburg, Incorporated, and has been surrounded by a wall. So long had the Powder Magazine stood without enclosure that all memory of the existence of one had been effaced. Williamsburgers were as much surprised as were the Restoration engineers when excavation uncovered the footings of a wall.

MARKET SQUARE TAVERN

Duke of Gloucester Street · No. 13 on Williamsburg map

ON THE southwest corner of Duke of Gloucester and Queen Streets is the restored Market Square Tavern, with its quaint old kitchen across the garden and its immaculate stable yard running south to Francis Street. The building was erected by John Dixon in 1749 for his residence and shop. Later Thomas Craig, a tailor, bought the property, enlarged it and opened an ordinary. Just prior to the Revolution, Gabriel Maupin, saddle and harness maker and keeper of the Powder Magazine, obtained the inn. After making additions and improvements, he carried on a successful hostelry business until 1802, when he sold the property to a Frenchman by the name of Peter Rob Deneufville. Forty years thereafter, the tavern was damaged by fire, but after repairs it continued to serve the public until the restoration of Colonial Williamsburg. Since its restoration, the old Market Square Tavern has resumed its ancient duties and is open to the public.

LIGHTFOOT HOUSE

Duke of Gloucester Street · *No. 14 on Williamsburg map*

LEAVING Market Square Tavern, passing several modern houses and crossing Queen Street, one reaches the Lightfoot House, a small square dwelling with gambrel roof. Opening on the entrance hall, which extends across the entire east end of the house, are the attractive living and dining rooms, both with interesting corner fireplaces. This little clapboard residence was built prior to 1748 by Philip Lightfoot, a wealthy lawyer and merchant of Yorktown. At his death, his son, William, inherited the home which remained in the Lightfoot family for almost a century. It has been restored to its pristine appearance, and, as all private Williamsburg residences, is not open to the public.

CAPTAIN ORR'S DWELLING

Duke of Gloucester Street · No. 15 on Williamsburg map

ON THE corner of Colonial and Duke of Gloucester Streets, separated by a low, white picket fence from the Lightfoot House, is Captain Orr's dwelling. This small and inviting story and a half, dormer cottage, with exposed brick chimneys, is shaded by lovely trees and flowering shrubs. In the rear is a lovely garden, a quaint smokehouse and interesting out-buildings.

There is no authentic date of the building of this old house nor is there much available information concerning it. During its restoration, archaeological and architectural examinations established the date of its erection prior to 1740. At that date it was occupied by Hugh Orr, a blacksmith. In 1771, this was the residence of James Southall, and during this year, tradition says, George Washington dined here. Early in the nineteenth century the dwelling was used as a tavern and was run by Robert Anderson.

BRICK HOUSE TAVERN

Duke of Gloucester and Botetourt Streets · No. 16 on Williamsburg map

LEAVING Captain Orr's dwelling, one passes the Orlando Jones house and office, the Mary Stith Shop, and the Nancy Camp House, before arriving at Doctor Carter's Brick House. Tradition and evidence from later deeds make it apparent that as early as 1723 Cole Digges owned this lot with a building thereon, and that during the ensuing thirty odd years his son, Dudley Digges, acquired and sold it. The first available deed to lead one to believe there was a large, substantial, brick house on this property, is dated March 16, 1761, when William Withers, a merchant, sells it to William Carter, an Apothecary. Doctor Carter subdivided the property and recorded a plot of the first floor and cellars. Shortly thereafter he sold the house and lot facing Francis Street to James Anderson, a blacksmith. The wooden shop, south of the large Brick house, facing Botetourt Street, was rented or sold to various persons during the remaining years of the eighteenth century. Among its many occupants of interest were William Cosby and Filmer Moore, who carried on the Riding-Chair-Maker's business, and "the sieur de Glovay," who drew plans of cities, counties and gentlemen's seats. The spacious Brick house, the advertisement which appeared in the Virginia Gazette of March 29, 1770, as under the management of Mary Davis. She was succeeded by Richard Hunt Singleton, who "determined to keep the best of Liquors and endeavour in every other respect to give satisfaction."

In 1842, practically every building on this entire block was destroyed by a disastrous fire. For many years after, the huge, brick gable ends of these houses stood sentinel over water filled foundations "that afforded the small boys rare sport—boating in the summer and skating in the winter."

BLAND-WETHERBURN HOUSE

Duke of Gloucester Street · No. 17 on Williamsburg map

CROSSING Botetourt Street and passing Tarpley's store, in today's language, Pender's, one reaches the Bland-Wetherburn House. Unlike most of the small square houses, this building is very long, has eight dormer windows in its gable roof and a lean-to on each side in the rear. The small pillared portico, of a later date than the house, is reached by steps on either side.

This notable dwelling was the home of Richard Bland, Senior. Under its roof, in 1710, according to tradition, was born Richard Bland, Junior, one of the most profound intellects of the revolutionary era. As the author of "An Enquiry into the Rights of the British Colonies," he laid down the doctrine widely applied since the Statute of Westminster that "America was no part of the kingdom of England, and was only united with it by the common tie of the crown."

Six years after the birth of this brilliant son, Richard Bland, Senior, sold the birthplace to Colonel Nathaniel Harrison of Wakefield, Surry County. About two decades later, Henry Wetherburn used the property as a tavern that must have been one of the finest in America. The inventory made after Wetherburn's death named each room in the house, the Bull Head Room, the Porch Chamber, the Middle Room, the Great Room, Mr. Page's Room, the Wheat Room, and so on. Details show that these quarters were supplied with much mahogany and walnut furniture, silver plate and glass ware.

The dwelling is privately owned and operated as an inn under the name of "Richard Bland Tavern."

CHARLTON'S INN

Duke of Gloucester Street · No. 18 on Williamsburg map

ADJOINING THE Bland-Wetherburn House is a charming private residence, once the renowned Charlton's Inn. The aforementioned Henry Wetherburn, that Eighteenth-century Oscar, bought from Nathaniel Harrison in 1738 this site and the lot on the west, "together with all houses." The famous Wetherburn Tavern was on the west lot. Charlton's Inn was next door. Bearing no resemblance to its neighbor, it is a square house with two full stories and a slanting roof. Thirty years later or thereabout, Richard Charlton owned and operated his well-known ordinary. Here it was that George Washington and other prominent Virginians stopped when visiting Williamsburg. After the Revolutionary War, another noted tavern keeper, Serafina Formicola, was manager. Shortly thereafter he moved to Richmond, where he established Formicola's Tavern, on the south side of east Main Street between Fifteenth and Seventeenth. A few years later he kept the fashionable Eagle Tavern on the same side of the same street near the southeast corner of Twelfth. Unlike Charlton's Inn, all traces of both these old Richmond Taverns have long since disappeared.

PURDIE'S DWELLING

Duke of Gloucester Street · No. 19 on Williamsburg map

SEPARATED from Charlton's Inn by an enclosed garden is the Purdie dwelling. This site was once the property of Colonel William Byrd of Westover, Charles City County, but so far as is known it never was occupied by a building that Byrd constructed or used. One of the earliest residents was Alexander Purdie, public printer of Virginia during the War of Independence, who occupied the house in 1767. His dwelling disappeared years ago but as the foundations remained intact, the Restoration, in 1930, built on them this quaint little story and a half residence with its single story additions and steep roof.

THE ROBERT'S HOUSE

Duke of Gloucester Street · *No. 20 on Williamsburg map*

ADJOINING THE lawn of the Purdie dwelling is a
two-story clapboard house with slanting shingled roof and center chimney. The residence is on the site of John Coke's Coffee House, which
was destroyed by fire five years prior to the War Between the States.
The dwelling was built by a Mr. Moss with the materials which survived the fire. Colonial Williamsburg, Incorporated, owns the property.

THE KERR HOUSE

Duke of Gloucester Street · No. 21 on Williamsburg map

AT THE east end of Duke of Gloucester Street on the southwest corner and opposite the Capitol is a large two and a half story brick residence. Its lovely lawn and interesting quarters are enclosed by an ivy covered brick wall. The original part of this house was built between 1707 and 1718 by William Robertson, lawyer and clerk of the Council of Colonial Virginia. He sold the property to Doctor John Brown and kept for his own residence the present Galt House on Francis Street. Doctor Brown was a noted physician and apothecary who had a valuable medical library, probably one of the most extensive in Virginia. After his death, Alexander Kerr, jeweler, goldsmith and silversmith, resided and had his shop here. In the early fall of 1736, he set up a brick kiln near his dwelling. This caused great annoyance to the Burgesses in the nearby Capitol, who ordered that the directors of the city of Williamsburg "take care to remove the nuisance of the said Brick-kiln that is preparing to be burnt near the Capitol." Kerr apparently lost his brick business but he continued to conduct lotteries —raffles they would be called now—which were drawn at his home. The prizes were elaborate snuff-boxes, chased gold and silver toothpick cases, rings set with jewels and cameos, handsome shoe buckles and other valuable articles of his craft. On his demise, the Virginia Gazette of October 20, 1738 pronounced him "a good Proficient in his Business and well respected—."

After Kerr, John Palmer, attorney and bursar of William and Mary College, resided here for a number of years. He married Elizabeth Lowe Tyler, aunt of Lewis and John Tyler, sometime judge and Governor of Virginia. To the old house, Vest built the eastern addition before the War Between the States. During the brief stay of General George B. McClellan in the town, ere he pressed on toward Richmond, this house served as his headquarters.

THE COLONIAL CAPITOL

East End of Duke of Gloucester Street · No. 22 on Williamsburg map

AT THE eastern terminus of Duke of Gloucester street, enclosed by a high brick wall and guarded by mulberry sentinels, is the stately second Capitol of the Old Dominion. This handsome building is a completely new structure, erected after much historical investigation and with the most painstaking regard for every ascertainable detail of the original edifice, which was the scene of much epochal legislation.

The association of the site with law-making dates from 1699, when the unhealthiness of Jamestown Island and the disrepair of the public buildings led the House of Burgesses to vote the removal of the Capitol to Williamsburg. Work authorized then was completed in 1705, although the new Capitol was occupied two years prior to this date. Its life was brief. Midwinter 1747, it was burned to the ground. Reconstructed within five years, it was the meeting place of the Burgesses and the Council until Williamsburg ceased to be the capital of Virginia. A tablet erected on the site by the Association for the Preservation of Virginia Antiquities, recorded a few of the many notable occurrences within the walls.

"THE OLD CAPITOL"

"Here Patrick Henry first kindled the flames of revolution by his resolutions and speech against the stamp act, May 29-30, 1765.

"Here March 12, 1773, Dabney Carr offered, and the House of Burgesses of Virginia unanimously adopted, the resolutions to appoint a committee to correspond with similar committees in other colonies—the first step taken towards the union of the States.

"Here May 15, 1776, the convention of Virginia, through resolutions drafted by Edmund Pendleton, offered by Thomas Nelson, Jr., advocated by Patrick Henry, unanimously called on Congress to declare the colonies free and independent States.

"Here, June 12, 1776, was adopted by the convention the immortal work of George Mason—the Declaration of Rights—and, on June 29, 1776, the first written constitution of a free and independent State ever framed."

Three years after the transfer of the seat of government to Richmond, the abandoned Capitol and grounds were vested in the City of Williamsburg. The municipality used it for a time as a school and permitted the students of George Wythe's law classes to hold their moot courts here. Like most public buildings in Williamsburg, it housed wounded soldiers of the Revolution. The Capitol was assigned to the French army, but after the burning of the Governor's Palace the American wounded shared the space. Later the historic Capitol served as a court house, but in 1832 it was again destroyed by fire. As that was before the use of photography, memory of the design of the building faded quickly. A Female Academy, built on the site, disappeared in time. The sacred ground subsequently passed to the Old Dominion Land Company, which in 1897 gave it to the Association for the Preservation of Virginia Antiquities.

When the restoration of Williamsburg was undertaken, the Association for the Preservation of Virginia Antiquities presented the land to Colonial Williamsburg, Incorporated. Employees of that organization conducted long investigations, gleaned many facts concerning the furniture of the Capitol and, at length, located in the Bodleian Library of Oxford an engraved copper plate that included a careful sketch of the building. On this basis, construction was carried forward. Now the Colonial Capitol stands recreated and resplendent. It is regarded as perhaps the nation's most faithful and brilliant example of the complete reconstruction of an historic building. As far as research could go, it reproduces the contents of the old structure, even to the difference between the "Council end" and the "Burgesses end" of the edifice. The Commonwealth of Virginia gratefully set the stamp of its approval on the reconstruction and, after dedicatory exercises on February 24, 1934, passed a resolution which permits the General Assembly to meet here one day each session. By act of the Assembly, an old stove built by order of Lord Botetourt for the Colonial House of Burgesses in Williamsburg and the chair of the Speaker of the House were brought back to the Capitol after remaining nearly one hundred and fifty years in Richmond.

The best and most interesting description of the original Capitol is to be found in the *"Present State of Virginia"* written in 1724 by the Reverend Hugh Jones, Master of Grammar School and Professor of Natural Philosophy and Mathematics at the College of William and Mary. His description is as follows:

"Fronting the College at near its whole Breadth, is extended a noble Street mathematically streight (for the first Design of the Town's Form is changed to a much better) just three Quarters of a Mile in Length: At the other End of which stands the Capitol, a noble, beautiful, and commodious Pile as any of its Kind, built at the Cost of the late Queen and by the Direction of the Governor. . . .

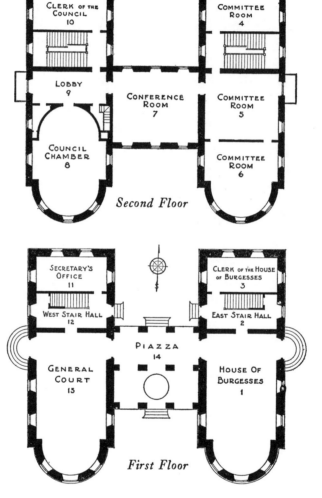

FLOOR PLANS OF THE RECONSTRUCTED CAPITOL
The rooms should be visited in the order indicated.

"The Building is in the Form of an H nearly; the Secretary's Office, and the General Court taking up one Side below Stairs; the Middle being an handsome Portico leading to the Clerk of the Assembly's Office, and the House of Burgesses on the other Side; which last is not unlike the House of Commons.

"In each Wing is a good Stair Case, one leading to the Council Chamber, where the Governor and Council sit in a very great State, in Imitation of the King and Council, or the Lord Chancellor and the House of Lords.

"Over the Portico is a large Room where Conferences are held, and Prayers are read by the Chaplain to the General Assembly; which Office I have had the Honour for some Years to perform. At one End of this is a Lobby, and near it is the Clerk of the Council's Office; and at the other End are several Chambers for the Committee of Claims, Privileges and Elections; and over all these are several good Offices for the Receiver General, for the Auditor, Treasurer, &c. and upon the Middle is raised a lofty Cupola with a large Clock. . . .

"The Cause of my being so particular in describing the Capitol is, because it is the best and most commodious Pile of its Kind that I have seen or heard of."

Well-informed Guides explain to all visitors the arrangement of rooms and the history of the paintings and decorations.

DOCTOR ROBERT WALLER HOUSE

Waller and Capitol Streets · No. 23 on Williamsburg map

LEAVING the Capitol and strolling across the eastern lawn to Waller Street, one sees in front the Royal Arms Inn, which is situated on the site of Williamsburg's second theatre, and on the left is a residence which has a long, long history. A survey of the property of Benjamin Waller, the first, was recorded in the York County records in April, 1749. In this survey, lots on the large tract of land which had been purchased by Waller from Mann Page were subdivided between the roads to Capitol Landing and to York Road. Part of the land east of the subdivision was developed into a park and grove and later was known as Waller's Grove. Here in the spring of 1776, after the adoption of the resolution proclaiming Virginia independent of Great Britain, a military parade and celebration were held. Brigadier-General Andrew Lewis received the troops; toasts were drunk, all made merry. On part of this estate stood Benjamin Waller's home, probably built many years before he purchased it and which long since has disappeared.

In the early part of the nineteenth century, Robert Waller resided here and had his "Doctor's Shop." The large frame dwelling house, with its two story back and front porches, was, for many years, the home of Captain Levin Winder Lane, Jr., former treasurer of the College of William and Mary.

THE COKE-GARRETT HOUSE

North of the Capitol on Nicholson Street

No. 24 on Williamsburg map

TURNING WEST at the corner of Capitol and Waller Streets and going down an incline, one approaches a charming, rambling residence known as the Coke-Garrett House. This house, once a tavern, was built about 1720, and is noted for its beautiful garden, which was long a landmark for locating other property. Twenty years after it was erected, it was bought by John Coke, goldsmith and jeweler, an ancestor of Richard Coke, one time United States Senator from Texas.

During the Revolutionary War, the dwelling was used for soldier's barracks. Subsequently, the property was purchased by the Garrett family in whose possession it remained for generations. The residence and inviting garden have been authentically restored. The interior as well as the exterior is charming. One enters from the west end which is the original part of the dwelling into a square hall with a rare old Chinese fretwork staircase. Opening on the hall is an informal study and a lovely drawing room. To reach the large and beautifully proportioned dining room with its panelled arches and mantel, one steps down a step from the drawing room. The entire house is furnished with carefully selected eighteenth century pieces.

THE PUBLIC GAOL

Nicholson Street · *No. 25 on Williamsburg map*

RELUCTANTLY leaving the lovely boxwood garden of the Coke-Garrett House, one inspects, at the foot of the hill on Nicholson Street, an ancient jail. The old "Public Gaol," a prison for the colony, was constructed shortly after the Capitol. An addition was made in 1711, as the General Court Prison for Debtors. Still later a house for the keeper was provided.

The building had many occupants, famous and infamous. In 1718 some of the pirates of the "Black-Beard" gang were imprisoned here before they were hanged on the road to Capitol Landing Creek, which is still known as "Gallows Road." Of more renowned persons, perhaps the most conspicuous was Henry Hamilton, Governor-General of Detroit, who was captured by General George Rogers Clark. During the War Between the States the old prison was partly destroyed by the Federal Troops. Later it was repaired, but after the building of the new jail it was never used again. The City of Williamsburg, which owned the prison, deeded it to Colonial Williamsburg, Incorporated.

The restored building represents the Public Gaol as it was in 1722-1773.

BRIDGET MENETRIE HOUSE

Nicholson Street · No. 26 on Williamsburg map

STOP A FEW moments at the tiny herb shop before climbing the hill up Nicholson Street, where, on the right hand side is the little story and a half white clapboard house, which was built in 1719 for Bridget Menetrie, a widow, who sold it the same year to Lewis Deloney. Twenty years thereafter it was the property of Andrew Anderson, a barber and peruke maker, who carried on his business here.

At present the property, which is privately owned, is styled "Redwood's Ordinary," but this is a misplaced name. The land was owned by Redwood in 1707, but his ordinary was immediately northeast of the Capitol, on Capitol Square.

PUBLIC RECORDS OFFICE

Adjoining the Capitol on Duke of Gloucester Street

No. 27 on Williamsburg map

RETRACING one's steps to the foot of the hill and climbing the incline leading to the Capitol, one passes the office of the Secretary of the Colony.

There are few records concerning this old brick building with its modern additions. It is believed to have been erected while the Capitol was being rebuilt after the fire of 1747. An account found in the Public Records Office, London, of His Majesty's Revenue of "Two s per hhd," arising within the Colony of Virginia from the 25th of April to the 25th of October, 1748, includes an item of £367: 19: 7, "the charge of a house built for the Public Records."

The building was used by the Secretary of the Colony as his office until the Capitol was moved to Richmond. Thereupon the City of Williamsburg provided that the District Court could be held here and that the former Secretary's office could be used as the Clerk's office.

Since the nineteenth century it has been a private residence.

THE RALEIGH TAVERN

Duke of Gloucester Street · No. 28 on Williamsburg map

BACK ON Duke of Gloucester Street going west one passes three privately owned colonial houses and two ancient ordinaries, the Sign of Edinburgh Castle and the Red Lion Inn.

The original Raleigh Tavern must have been built prior to 1742, for in that year the property was sold by John Blair to an operating company which employed Henry Wetherburn, of "Arrack Punch" fame, as keeper. During the following thirty odd years it was owned or occupied by John Dixon and Company, Alexander Finnie, John Chiswell and George Gilmer, William Trebell, Anthony Hay and James Barret Southall. Under all these successive managers, the tavern proved the chosen meeting place for patriotic gatherings, for banquets and for gay assemblies. Potentates occasionally lodged there.

The House of Burgesses met here in 1773 after being dissolved and denied the use of the Capitol by Lord Dunmore for aiding in the arduous struggle for liberty.

The Phi Beta Kappa Society is believed to have been organized in the Apollo Hall of the tavern in the turbulent days of 1776. Here the Society held its annual anniversaries until the end of the Revolution.

Still another notable event, among many, was staged on February 22, 1779, when "a very elegant entertainment was given at the Raleigh Tavern by the inhabitants of Williamsburg to celebrate the anniversary of the birth of General George Washington, Commander-in-Chief of the army of the United States, the savior of his country and the brave assister of the rights and liberties of mankind."

The famous old tavern was destroyed by fire in 1859. On its site rose modern stores which, with their successors, remained until 1930. In that year the Colonial Williamsburg, Incorporated, rebuilt the ancient hostelry on the original foundation, according to plans based on public records, manuscripts and old prints. The building has been furnished authentically in accordance with its early inventories and is open to the public.

199

THE PRENTIS HOUSE

Duke of Gloucester Street · *No. 29 on Williamsburg map*

TAKING LEAVE of the famous old Raleigh Tavern, one passes the Sign of the Golden Ball, Metalsmiths and Pewters, before reaching the large, story and a half, white clapboard house with dark chocolate blinds and slate roof, known as the Prentis House. In the side rear are several much smaller dwellings and a stable, all surrounding "a well-managed kitchen garden." Between 1712 and 1714, John Brooke erected a house on this lot and within the ensuing ten years sold the small dwelling, fronting west, to his son-in-law, William Prentis. Brooke continued to live on the premises until his death in 1729. He bequeathed his house and lots to his wife for her life and afterwards to his daughter, Mary Prentis, and her heirs, and in default of such heirs, to William Prentis and his heirs forever. Thirty-six years thereafter, at the death of William Prentis, he left to his wife "that part of the lot whereon I now live, which was conveyed to me by my father-in-law, Mr. Brooke," and the remainder to his sons. This residue must have included the spacious residence facing Duke of Gloucester Street, which in the seventeen-nineties was insured by Mathew Anderson. In 1826 it was inherited by Robert Anderson, an extensive property owner in Williamsburg.

The buildings on this property are believed to have been destroyed by fire in 1842, and their reconstruction has just been completed.

PITT-DIXON HOUSE

Duke of Gloucester Street · No. 30 on Williamsburg map

CROSSING Botetourt Street, one passes the Davidson Shop, once the apothecary shop of Doctor Robert Davidson, an early Mayor of Williamsburg, now a grocery and hardware store; next door the Teterel Shop displays its wares, then a few steps and over a low fence one views the site of William Parks' Printing Office, the birthplace of the Virginia Gazette. One has now reached the northeast corner of Colonial Street and the charming little yellow frame dwelling, with slanting roof and olive green shutters, whose entrance is guarded by two large honeysuckle bushes.

As early as 1718 there were two buildings on this lot, but it was not until 1729, after several transfers, that Richard Packe bought the property. His widow kept a millinery shop and rented rooms to lodgers. After her marriage to Doctor George Pitt, he kept his apothecary shop, under the name of "The Sign of the Rhinoceros," in the eastern portion of the dwelling. Two years after Mrs. Pitt's death, which occurred in 1772, Doctor Pitt sold the houses to John Dixon, guardian of young William Hunter, whose printing office adjoined. During the Revolution, William Hunter, being a loyalist, acted as a British spy, later joining the army under Cornwallis at Yorktown. His property, as shown by the Public Records Office, London, was confiscated by the Commonwealth.

This attractive little residence, whose reconstruction has lately been completed was destroyed by a fire about 1896 when most of the other buildings on the block shared alike.

DOCTOR ARCHIBALD BLAIR'S APOTHECARY SHOP

Duke of Gloucester Street · *No. 31 on Williamsburg map*

CROSSING Colonial Street, one is in front of a little house at one time Doctor Blair's medicine store. The gable end of this small building facing Duke of Gloucester Street now displays fascinating old wigs and intricate wares of the ancient peruke maker. The four dormer windows are equally divided on each side of its peaked roof, while the outside brick chimney is in the rear. This property was deeded to Doctor Archibald Blair by the trustees of the city in the first year of the eighteenth century, and in a record of a few years later, mention is made of a house on the lot, possibly the present structure. Here, for many years, Doctor Blair kept his shop. After his death it remained in his family for decades. During a part of their ownership, the little brick building was occupied by James Carter, also an apothecary. Not until the late eighteen hundreds was it used for other business. Today it is a "Barber and Peruke Maker's exhibition shop of Colonial Williamsburg, Incorporated."

THE LUDWELL-PARADISE HOUSE

Duke of Gloucester Street · No. 32 on Williamsburg map

IN THE MIDDLE of the same square with the tiny apothecary shop and in great contrast to it, is the stately brick residence known as the Ludwell-Paradise House.

Philip Ludwell, the second, of Greenspring, James City County, acquired this and adjoining lots in September, 1700, and subsequently erected this large house, which passed in time to his granddaughter, Lucy Ludwell. In 1769, she married John Paradise, son of Peter Paradise, formerly British consul at Thessalonica, Greece. The two lived here for a short time and then went to England. Paradise and his wife became close friends of Samuel Johnson, who visited their home frequently and wrote them often. Numerous references to their association with the lexicographer will be found in George Birkbeck's fine edition of Boswell's "Johnson."

During the Revolution, the Virginia property of Mrs. Paradise was confiscated because her husband was regarded as a British subject. On October 26, 1779, Mr. and Mrs. Paradise petitioned the House of Delegates for the return of the property on the ground that the estate was held in the right of the wife and that John Paradise was a native of Greece and should not come under the operation of the escheat law for British subjects.

The property was finally restored to Mr. and Mrs. Paradise who returned to this country for four years after the Revolution. Toward the close of the century, they again crossed the Atlantic to England, where Mr. Paradise died. His widow came back to Virginia and lived in the state until her death in 1814. Mr. and Mrs. Paradise had two children, Portia, who died young, and Lucy, who married Count Philip Barziza.

Because of its interesting historical associations and charming architectural background, the Paradise residence has been restored with much care. Here one may see Mrs. John D. Rockefeller, Jr.'s Loan Collection of American Folk Art.

BLAIR'S BRICK HOUSE

Duke of Gloucester Street · No. 33 on Williamsburg map

ADJOINING the Ludwell-Paradise House is another substantial brick residence called Blair's Brick House, which since its restoration has been used as an antique shop of Eighteenth Century English pieces. In the rear of this gracious dwelling is a lovely lawn and ancient trees.

The lot on which the house stands was a part of the original grant, in 1700, to Philip Ludwell, the second, of Green Spring and builder of the before mentioned Ludwell-Paradise House. Ludwell, having failed to build on this land within twenty-four months, forfeited the property which escheated to the trustees of the city. In 1725, John Blair bought the lots from Robert Cobbs and, in his will recorded on October 5, 1771, bequeathed them to his son, John Blair, and his heirs forever. The remaining years of its existence and final disappearance are very vague and in 1928 the property was deeded to Doctor W. A. R. Goodwin as an unimproved lot.

THE COURT HOUSE OF 1770

(Williamsburg-James City Court House)

Duke of Gloucester Street · No. 34 on Williamsburg map

CROSSING Queen Street, one walks west on Duke of Gloucester to the middle of the block where, on Market Square, facing south England Street, is the old Court House. The genesis of this famous structure is recorded by the Virginia Gazette of March 23, 1769 in these words:

"The Common Hall having this day determined to build a commodious brick courthouse in this city and having appointed us to agree with and undertake to build the same, we do hereby give notice that we shall meet at Mr. Hay's (Raleigh Tavern) on Tuesday, the 4th of April, to let the building thereof; we are also appointed to dispose of the present courthouse, and the grounds on which the same stands. James Cocke, James Carter, John Carter, John Tazewell.

"N. B. The plan of the above Court House may be seen at Mr. Hay's at any time."

The courthouse was built the following year, during Governor Norborne Berkeley's administration, and long was used for hearings and trials. Perhaps the most notable single event within its walls was the formal proclamation by Governor Benjamin Harrison of the Treaty of Peace in 1783.

The courthouse housed a multitude of public records, many of which had the largest historical interest. During the War Between the States, the more valuable of these papers were sent to Richmond for safe-keeping. Unfortunately, in the "Evacuation Fire" of April 3, 1865, they were burned. At the beginning of the second decade of the twentieth century, the courthouse itself was greatly damaged by flames, but no further loss of records occurred. The building, duly repaired, continued in use until the restoration of Williamsburg. Then it was transferred to Colonial Williamsburg and was set aside as a museum. Here one may trace, step by step, the fascinating archaeology of the restoration as shown in countless articles and scraps of materials found in the excavation of over a hundred foundations.

THE NORTON HOUSE

Duke of Gloucester Street · No. 35 on Williamsburg map

A FEW FEET off Duke of Gloucester Street, facing Market Square, is the Norton House. This dwelling is an architectural enigma. It has characteristics of the early Republican period of architecture, which probably was superimposed on a colonial house. The historical records show that a building, either brick or wood, was built here about 1718. It was not until fifty years later, when James Patterson here kept a shop where he repaired "horizontal, plain and repeating watches and clocks," that the building was described as a "Brick House," opposite Mr. Baker's.

During the years between, it was owned by James Geddy, gunsmith and jeweler; James Taylor, a tailor, and the noted merchant, Hugh Walker. Doctor Andrew Anderson, surgeon of New Kent County, at one time lived here. He was followed by Bartholomew le Petit, who kept a school at the "Brick House."

During the Revolutionary War, the dwelling was purchased by John Hatley Norton, a young merchant who married Sally Nicholas, daughter of Robert Carter Nicholas, Treasurer of the Colony. Ten years before the turn of the twentieth century, Bathurst Daingerfield Peachy bought the property. In 1930, the residence was renovated, at which time the modern additions were demolished and the lead colored paint over the beautiful old bricks was removed. The property is owned by Colonial Williamsburg, Incorporated, and is occupied by a descendant of the Peachy family.

THE JAMES GEDDY HOUSE

Duke of Gloucester Street and Palace Green · No. 36 on Williamsburg map

ON THE CORNER of Duke of Gloucester Street, facing the Travis House, is a lovely old square two-story clapboard dwelling. A white picket fence separates an inviting boxwood garden from Market Square on the east and Palace Green on the west. The residence is an interesting example of the manner in which some Williamsburg houses have been so changed by successive owners that the character of the original structure has been modified or, in some instances, lost. As early as 1716 there were buildings on this lot. Two and twenty years later, James Geddy, jeweler and gunsmith, bought the house from Samuel Boush and his wife, Frances. He and his sons after him lived here and carried on his trade during most of the eighteenth century. At one time the dwelling was owned by the Bucktrout family. Still other names occur in the deeds. By some, if not by all, of these owners, additions and architectural changes were made. The present restored house consequently is of a much later appearance than the probable date of the original construction would indicate.

GRIFFIN-COLEMAN HOUSE

Nicholson and Queen Streets · No. 37 on Williamsburg map

TURNING the corner of Duke of Gloucester Street and going north along Palace Green, one enjoys the charming garden of the Geddy House. Reaching the end of the square, one travels east on Nicholson Street to the Ludwell-Paradise stables opposite which is the Griffin-Coleman House. This clapboard, dormer-windowed dwelling was built, on a very much smaller scale, by Francis Tyler in 1717. Subsequently, Benjamin Waller made additions and improvements. In 1759, it was the town residence of John Tayloe, of Mount Airy, Richmond County. Judge Cyrus Griffin, the last president of the Continental Congress and the first judge of the District Court of the United States for Virginia, resided here with his wife, Lady Christina Steuart of Scotland, daughter of the sixth Earl of Traquair. Tradition has it, also, that about the second year of the nineteenth century, William Wirt, the celebrated lawyer and author, lived here while serving as Chancellor of Virginia.

After the War Between the States, this property belonged to the Coleman family, who sold it to Colonial Williamsburg, Incorporated.

THE RANDOLPH-PEACHY HOUSE

Nicholson and England Streets facing Market Square

No. 38 on Williamsburg map

RETRACING our way to the Palace Green, one pauses in passing to view several very interesting old residences. At the northeast corner of Nicholson and England Streets is the Randolph-Peachy House. Here is a property associated with renowned names and mentioned in the records as early as November 11, 1714, when the trustees of the City of Williamsburg deeded eight lots to William Robertson with the proviso that he finish one or more good dwelling houses on the tract within twenty-four months or else return the whole to the city. These lots covered the entire square bounded by Nicholson, England, Scotland and Queen Streets. Robertson must have met the condition of the deed, because, within nine years, he sold four lots to John Holloway with houses and windmill. From these four lots John Holloway transferred to John Randolph "Lot or half acre of land lying and being in the City of Williamsburg, adjoining to the lot whereon the said John Randolph now lives, which the said John Holloway purchased of William Robertson."

At Sir John Randolph's death this property passed to his eldest son, Peyton, who became Speaker of the House of Burgesses, first President of the first Continental Congress and three times President of the Virginia Convention in 1774 and 1775.

Under the will of his wife, Mrs. Betty Randolph, the property was sold at public auction. Two years after the Revolution, Joseph Hornsby bought it.

This residence, which had been visited by both Lafayette and Rochambeau, was later acquired by Thomas Griffin Peachy. From the Peachy family the property passed to the Hansfords, in whose possession it remained until several years after the War Between the States. Toward the close of the century, Edmund W. Warburton, Mayor of Williamsburg, resided here. The house is privately owned.

THE ARCHIBALD BLAIR HOUSE

Nicholson and England Streets facing Market Square

No. 39 on Williamsburg map

ENCLOSED BY a white picket fence and shaded by two towering crape myrtle trees is the lovely old two-story clapboard dwelling, built, prior to 1719, by Doctor Archibald Blair. He must have loved flowers, for, as early as 1723, he so had adorned the grounds of his home that lots were described in deeds as adjoining "the garden of Archibald Blair."

After Doctor Blair's death the property passed to the noted surgeon and apothecary, Doctor Peter Hay. His widow, Grizzle Hay, kept lodgers, among whom, tradition has it, Patrick Henry was to be counted when in attendance on the sessions of the House of Burgesses. The residence was again owned by a Blair when John Blair purchased it of Doctor Gilmer, who had bought it from the executors of the Hay estate. Toward the end of the Revolutionary War, when the President's house on the college campus was seized by Cornwallis and later used by the officers of the French army, Bishop James Madison and his family occupied this house as their residence. Later this was the home of the Reverend James Henderson, Master of the Grammar School and son-in-law of John Blair, President of the Council.

THE ST. GEORGE TUCKER HOUSE
THE LEVINGSTON HOUSE and
SITE OF THE FIRST THEATRE
IN AMERICA

Nicholson Street and Palace Green · *No. 40 on Williamsburg map*

ADJOINING THE garden of Archibald Blair on Nicholson Street and facing Market Square is the fascinating, long and rambling residence of the distinguished Tucker family. The main part of this lovely and interesting old white clapboard dwelling is two full stories high, flanked by tall red brick chimneys, on either side of which are twin story and a half wings, with peaked roofs and dormer windows. On the west, or the Palace Green side of the residence is another quaint one and a half story building with a huge outside chimney and connected with the big house by an enclosed passageway. The interior with its soft toned ancestral portraits and lovely English antiques is even more attractive than the charming exterior. This should be a shrine for Thespians, because it carries the American theatre back two centuries and more.

On November 5, 1716, William Levingston leased three half-acre lots on Palace Street from the Trustees of the City of Williamsburg for a period of five hundred years. He promptly made an agreement with Charles Stagg, a dancing master and Mary Stagg, his wife, to erect thereon a suitable play house. Stagg procured subscriptions from thirty-one prominent Virginians and, in less than two years, completed the theatre, a dwelling house, a kitchen and a bowling green. The playhouse was more readily built than patronized. Five years after leasing the property, Levingston mortgaged it to Archibald Blair, who later acquired it and bequeathed it in time to John Blair. By him, the tract and improvements were sold to Doctor George Gilmer, builder of the apothecary shop on the corner of Nicholson and Palace Streets.

The theatre, having been unused for a number of years, had fallen into ruin. Citizens of Williamsburg petitioned the "gentlemen subscribers to the playhouse 'to present the building to the town for a Common Hall.' " As the subscribers were obliging, the title to the

223

structure passed to the Mayor and Aldermen of the City. Doctor Gilmer deeded them the ground on which the theatre stood with six feet around it. Repairs to the playhouse were ordered immediately, but it prospered no more as a Common Hall than as a theatre. Sometime after December 1745, it became the Hustings Court House and so remained for the next twenty-five years until the joint James City County-Williamsburg Court House was erected on the Market Square green.

The property passed through various hands until John Tazewell claimed that the five hundred year lease of William Levingston was not transferable because Levingston had died without issue. Governor Dunmore, on August 1, 1772, upheld the contention and granted the three lots to John Tazewell for £3 of tobacco. Tazewell purchased the rights to the buildings and lots from all the other owners, and finally sold the whole to William Rowsay, who deeded it to Edmund Randolph. On July 3, 1788, Randolph conveyed it to St. George Tucker, who erected the present house. There is a theory that some of the old buildings, and perhaps even the theatre itself, were incorporated into the dwelling. This theory seems supported by strong architectural evidence.

The residence and garden, which are owned by Colonial Williamsburg, Incorporated, have been restored and are occupied by descendants of St. George Tucker, professor of law and outstanding author. The site of the original theatre, which adjoins the charming and symmetrical boxwood garden and faces the Palace Green, was presented to Colonial Williamsburg, Incorporated, by Mayor and Mrs. George P. Coleman.

THE BRUSH HOUSE

Palace Green · No. 41 on Williamsburg map

IF THE spirit of old-time actors walk the site of the old theatre and Levingston's House, dancers must haunt the nearby Brush House which nestles behind ancient lilacs and where climbing roses run riot up the slender columns to the upstairs porch. John Brush, gunsmith and armorer to Governor Spotswood, accepted a deed to two lots from the Trustees of the City of Williamsburg in 1717 on condition that he build on the property within two years. The condition was duly met, the existing house was erected and in time was inherited by John's daughter Elizabeth Brush, spinster. It passed in the course of years through various hands to William Dering, the dancing master. This worthy had advertised in 1737 through the Virginia Gazette that he had opened a Dancing School at the College of William and Mary, "where all Gentlemen's Sons may be taught Dancing, according to the newest French manner." He conducted Dancing and Balls at the Capitol during the sittings of the General Court for a number of years, but disaster must have come to him. Two years after purchasing the little dwelling, he mortgaged it, the furniture, his riding horse and slaves to Peter Hay and Bernard Moore. The following year the house and property was again mortgaged, this time to Philip Lightfoot, who subsequently acquired title and rented the place to a succession of tenants. Tradition affirms, although there is no record, that this was the town lodging of Governor John Page of Rosewell, Gloucester County, a member of the Convention of 1776, Colonel in the Revolutionary War, representative in Congress and later Governor of Virginia. As the legend runs, Governor Page's widow and his daughter, Lucy, who became Mrs. Robert Saunders, were living here when Lafayette visited Williamsburg in 1824.

Two years before the middle of the nineteenth century, Sydney Smith purchased the property. It is still owned and occupied by his descendants. The original garden, with its old-fashioned flowers, shrubs and dwarf box and the fascinating story and a half rooi dence, with the much later two-story porch, hold a charm all their own. Two window panes bear old inscriptions, on one is scratched A. Bushe, 1734; on the other S. B. 1796—O fatal day.

227

THE GOVERNOR'S PALACE

End of the Palace Green Facing South · No. 42 on Williamsburg map

THIS MOST splendid of all the buildings of the Williamsburg Restoration rests on the foundations and basement of a Governor's House which the Burgesses of Virginia somewhat tardily constructed after the removal of the Capitol from Jamestown. Authorized in 1705, it was incomplete in 1710, but by 1723 the Reverend Hugh Jones, Master of Grammar School and Professor of Natural Philosophy and Mathematics at William and Mary College, was able to proclaim it "a magnificient structure, finished and beautified with gates, fine gardens, offices, walks, a fine canal, orchards, etc." The construction was under the direction of Henry Cary, who also was overseer of the Capitol. His son, Henry Cary, built the President's House on the campus of William and Mary College.

All the Colonial Governors from Alexander Spotswood onward resided here. When Republican ways prevailed, neither the first Governor of the Commonwealth, Patrick Henry, nor the Second, Thomas Jefferson, disdained such comforts as the Palace afforded. Soon after Jefferson went to Richmond, on the second removal of the Capitol, the Palace had new occupants—the sick and wounded American soldiers who had participated in the Siege of Yorktown. Their residence was brief, for the Palace caught fire and burned to the ground. The patients were moved to the other hospitals in town, occupied by the French. Only one soldier perished in the flames, but on the Palace grounds are buried over a hundred soldiers of the War of Independence.

Although the center walls of the Palace remained after the fire, the main structure was not rebuilt. The bricks finally were sold by the State. Two flanking offices, which had escaped the fire, were used as residences until the War Between the States, when they, too, were destroyed. In time a public school was erected where the Palace had reared its proud walls, but this was demolished that the Palace might be reconstructed. As in the case of the Capitol, the "copperplate" in the Bodleian was the basis of the plan for the reconstruction. Ground plans by Jefferson, in the keeping of the Massachusetts Historical Society aided

greatly, as did the old foundations and the numerous inventories made for successive Governors. There is every reason to believe that the present structure accurately duplicates the old Palace. Whether the buildings ever were furnished in Colonial days as exquisitely as they now are, one may be permitted to doubt. As it stands today, the Palace is a museum of noble antiques, a permanent exhibit in the most gracious interior decorating and in flawless landscape architecture. The Palace with its beautiful surroundings are open to the public. Here, as at the Capitol, costumed guides conduct the visitors.

THE CARTER-SAUNDERS HOUSE

Palace Green · No. 43 on Williamsburg map

RELUCTANTLY closing the heavy entrance gate to the Palace and turning to view the restful beauty of Palace Green, one sees in the distance, above towering trees, the graceful steeple of old Bruton Church. Following the top of the high ivy-covered brick wall of the churchyard, one's gaze returns to the ancient mulberry trees on the west side of the Green. Here is the spacious and elegant residence known as the Carter-Saunders House. This house is constructed of clapboard painted white and is two full stories in height, with small, one story, one room wings. Flanking both wings is a white picket fence enclosing a beautiful lawn and enchanting garden. Few private dwellings in Williamsburg have so many distinguished names associated with them as this charming old residence on Palace Green. Built early in the eighteenth century, it was owned at one time by Charles Carter of King George County and later, during the repair of the Palace, was occupied by Governor Robert Dinwiddie. Later owners included Philip Grymes, "His Majesty's Receiver General," and Robert Carter Nicholas, Treasurer of the Colony, Speaker of the House of Burgesses and son of Elizabeth Carter, widow of Major Nathaniel Burwell, and wife of Doctor George Nicholas, of Lancaster County, England. From Robert Carter Nicholas the dwelling passed to his cousin, Robert Carter of Nomini Hall, central figure in the charming diary of Philip Fithian. After "Councillor Carter's" day, the property was acquired by Robert Saunders, whose son of the same name, President of William and Mary College, in the eighteen-forties, married Lucy, daughter of Governor John Page. They too resided here.

THE DEANE HOUSE

Palace Green · No. 44 on Williamsburg map

STROLLING SOUTH on Palace Green, one stops at the corner of Prince George Street to view the exterior of another lately reconstructed stately residence. The first record of the property is in the summer of 1720, when the trustees of the city deeded it to John Holloway with the usual building clause, therefore it is assumed that this large dwelling and the kitchen were erected soon thereafter. In 1772, Doctor William Carter, the surgeon, who had lived here for several years, sold the house with its lovely garden, lawn and quarters to Elkanah Deane, famous Dublin coach-maker who came from New York under the patronage of the royal governor, John Murray, Earl of Dunmore. It was Deane who built the Forge and Shop which one may visit at the foot of the hill on Prince George Street. Here one will find a blacksmith in eighteenth century apparel forging with old tools copies of wrought iron hardware of colonial days.

The Deane Shop and Forge must not have proved a success for within four years it is advertised that William Holladay has taken Elkanah Deane's Shop, where he will carry on the coachmaking business.

There does not seem to be any record concerning these buildings after their appearance on the Frenchman's Map, although legend has their existence up to the War Between the States.

THE GEORGE WYTHE HOUSE

Palace Green   :   No. 45 on Williamsburg map

RETRACING the way up the hill, one stops to visit the last house of historic interest on Palace Green, the staunch old Wythe House, weathered and mellow, and by every test, one of the half-dozen most famous buildings of Williamsburg. It was built in 1755 for Richard Taliaferro, a "most skillful architect," to whom had been intrusted, a few years previously, the extensive repairs and additions to the Governor's Palace. The house passed in 1775 from Taliaferro, who doubtless drew the plans, to his celebrated son-in-law, Chancellor George Wythe. Wythe was the first professor of law at William and Mary College, one of the Signers of the Declaration of Independence, and had the unique distinction of counting among his pupils two Presidents of the United States, Jefferson and Monroe, and the great Chief Justice, John Marshall. These three men and others almost as renowned doubtless visited this house often. George Washington occupied the residence as his headquarters during the closing months of the Revolutionary War.

The property passed through numerous hands, but escaped serious fire and injury in the long, chequered history of Williamsburg. Finally, in 1926, the Colonial Dames of America, Chapter Number Three, presented the building to Bruton Parish Church. The Reverend W. A. R. Goodwin, D.D., then rector of that famous church, raised money for its renovation and had as his consultants in the restoration R. T. H. Halsey and Charles O. Cornelius of the American Wing of the Metropolitan Museum. In its reclaimed dignity, the building was used by Bruton Church as a parish house until 1937, when the vestry sold it to Colonial Williamsburg, Incorporated, who have removed the modern additions and restored its former elegance.

BRUTON PARISH CHURCH

Duke of Gloucester Street and Palace Green

No. 46 on Williamsburg map

ADJOINING the stately Wythe mansion is historic Bruton Parish Church, which has served continuously longer than any Episcopal Church in America. Established in 1614 or 1615 as Harrop Parish, it remained as such for forty odd years when it was added to "Middle Plantation" and called "Middletown Parish," but not until 1674 did it become "Bruton Parish." At that date the church was a wooden edifice built on the land given by Colonel John Page, a member of the Colonial Council. This little house of worship was substituted, in nine years, by a brick structure, the predecessor of the present church, which was erected between 1710 and 1715 on the original site.

Between 1905-07, the interior was extensively repaired through the efforts and under the supervision of its far-seeing rector, the late Reverend W. A. R. Goodwin, D.D. Many years later, when serving his second rectorship in this parish, he conceived the vision of a restored Williamsburg, and through him Mr. Rockefeller became interested and together they dreamed dreams which are now realities. Again in 1938, under the direction of Doctor Goodwin, the old brick church was restored to its original appearance and the ivy and stained glass windows removed.

Among the interesting and valuable possessions within these hallowed walls are the Parish register of 1632, the stone font, still in use and said to have been imported eight years after the erection of the first brick church, and the three silver communion services—"The Jamestown Service," given to the Church at Jamestown in 1661 by Colonel Francis Moryson, Deputy or Lieutenant-Governor at that time; "The College Service," given to William and Mary College in 1775 by Lady Rebecca Stanton Gooch, wife of Sir William Gooch, one time Lieutenant-Governor, and "The Bruton Parish Service," which bears the Arms of England during the reign of George, the third, and thought to be a gift of Francis Fauquier, Lieutenant-Governor, who is buried in the north aisle of the present church.

THE BLAIR HOUSE

Duke of Gloucester Street · No. 47 on Williamsburg map

HEADING WEST on Duke of Gloucester Street, one passes The Armistead House, a large red brick residence of the eighteen-fifty period built by Lemuel J. Bowden, a lawyer. On the next square, adjoining the new Parish House, is the interesting old home of John Blair, Senior, President of the Council. This quaint story and a half house, with a large brick chimney at each end of its dormer windowed roof and two front entrances, was built for him between 1745 and 1747. On the east side of the dwelling, facing a quaint, symmetrical herb garden is the fascinating old gabled roof kitchen with its huge outside chimney. Later his son, John Blair, Junior, Justice of the Supreme Court, resided here. Traditionally, too, John Marshall lodged here while studying law at William and Mary College under George Wythe. In the last decade of the eighteenth century, the property was owned by Robert Andrews, husband of Mary Blair, daughter of John Blair, Junior. Robert Andrews was instructor of Mathematics at William and Mary College and Secretary to Thomas Nelson, Governor of the Colony.

THE MINOR HOUSE

Prince George and Nassau Streets · No. 48 on Williamsburg map

ON BOTH SIDES of Duke of Gloucester Street, between the John Blair House and William and Mary College, are the previously mentioned new shop buildings, of Tidewater Virginia Colonial design, constructed by the Williamsburg Restoration as a business area for the town. Unless there is shopping to be done, the rest of one's journey can best be seen by motor. Starting at the corner of Duke of Gloucester and Nassau Streets, the path leads north to Prince George Street. Here, on the southwest corner, almost hid by a beautiful weeping willow, is a small frame house of the Early Republic type built a few years before the War Between the States. This was the residence of Lucian Minor, professor of law at William and Mary College. Later John S. Charles, one of Williamsburg's oldest and most respected citizens, owned and occupied the dwelling for forty years. He was the author of valuable recollections of Williamsburg and President of the Pulaski Club until his death in 1930. The little residence is privately occupied and has not been restored.

THE TIMSON HOUSE

Prince George and Nassau Streets · No. 49 on Williamsburg map

ACROSS the road from the Minor dwelling and guarded by stately maples, is an inconspicuous little abode known as the Timson House. Not all of Colonial Williamsburg was "pomp and circumstance," nor are all its surviving houses great mansions. Here, to be specific, is an humble house built at an unascertained date prior to May 31, 1717, when James Shields bought it from William Timson. Subsequently, it was the home of a bricklayer, William Pegram, and then the abode of James Wray, a master carpenter and one of the builders appointed to direct the remodelling of the Governor's Palace in the middle of the eighteenth century. Tradition has it that this was one of the many houses in which French troops were billeted during the campaign of 1781.

On the property was a spring which for years supplied the neighborhood with water. After the War Between the States, an old female occupant of the house kept cows which were allowed to graze over the greens and open lots of the town. As she dealt in the produce of their browsing, the place acquired the name of "Buttermilk Hill," which it still has among old Williamsburgers.

WHEATLAND

Henry and Scotland Streets · *No. 50 on Williamsburg map*

TRAVELING WEST on Prince George Street, there are no places of historic interest until reaching Henry Street; here one turns north and sees at the end of the square, back from the road in the shade of old trees, the former residence of William Holt, Mayor of Williamsburg and builder of the house. He purchased the property from James Carter at the close of the Revolutionary War. Wheatland, as it has been known for many years, is a large, two story, wooden dwelling with double verandas and later additions. It is situated on a part of what was originally a grant of two hundred and fifty acres of land deeded in 1652 to Henry Tyler, the first of the name and forefather of John Tyler, Governor of Virginia, and his son, John, tenth President of the United States. Fifty odd years later a portion of the estate was sold for the site of the Governor's Palace.

Wheatland is a private residence and not within the area of Colonial Williamsburg, Incorporated.

THE GRIFFIN HOUSE

Francis Street · No. 51 on Williamsburg map

DRIVING WEST on Scotland Street to Boundary Street, one turns left, crosses Duke of Gloucester Street, passes the entrance to William and Mary College and keeps on one more square to Francis Street. Here on the southeast corner is an ivy-covered, red-brick, dormer dwelling built before 1776. Subsequently it was the property of Doctor Samuel Griffin, who served his state as a member of the House of Delegates and later as a Representative in Congress. Here resided, also, the widow of William Trebell Galt, the former Mayor of Williamsburg and superintendent of the Eastern State Hospital. At one time, Doctor Richard A. Wise, son of Henry Alexander Wise, Governor of Virginia, had his home under the old roof. Five years before the end of the nineteenth century, Miss Maria Marshall owned and occupied the residence.

The house is the property of Colonial Williamsburg, Incorporated.

THE CUSTIS KITCHEN

Eastern State Hospital Grounds

Francis Street · No. 52 on Williamsburg map

DRIVING EAST on Francis Street, one pauses after passing the entrance to the Eastern State Hospital. Here, on the crest of the hill beneath towering old trees, is the small whitewashed brick kitchen with its lone chimney, the last remaining building of at least five others which once comprised the magnificent Custis plantation. About 1714, on this land, later to be known as the "six-chimney lot," Colonel John Custis, wealthy planter and aristocrat, erected one of Williamsburg's handsomest residences, surrounding his mansion with beautiful gardens and pleasant walkways. At his death, thirty-five years thereafter, his son, Daniel Parke Custis, first husband of Martha Washington, inherited the famous estate. Unfortunately, after years of neglect the stately old residence fast fell to ruin. Subsequently the property became the Eastern State Hospital.

Virtually all the numerous buildings of this large State hospital for the mentally sick are comparatively modern, but the institution itself dates from 1769. At the session of that year, the General Assembly of Virginia appointed a committee to arrange an asylum "for the reception of idiots, lunatics and other persons of unsound mind." This seems to have been the first legislative provision in America for the public care of the insane, though small private institutions may have existed before that time. Robert Smith, of Philadelphia, drew the plans, which Benjamin Powell executed. On September 14, 1773, the Hospital was completed. James Galt was the first superintendent, with Doctor John de Sequeyra as physician in charge. A month later the first patient was admitted. In 1885 the original buildings were burned.

TAZEWELL HALL

South England Street · No. 53 on Williamsburg map

DOWN ONE HILL and up another, passing the new Court House which is on the site of the First Colonial Court House, one turns right at England street where just south of the Williamsburg Lodge stands Tazewell Hall. This massive two and a half story frame house, with various additions and many chimneys, was originally at the southern terminus of England street, but early in the twentieth century, when England street was extended south, it was moved to its present location on the west side of the street. This elegant old mansion was the home of John Randolph, the last Royal Attorney General for Virginia and the birthplace of Edmund Randolph, his son, the first Attorney General and Secretary of State of the United States. Traditionally it is said that John disinherited Edmund for refusing to adhere to the royal cause. John Randolph, "the Tory," cast his lot with Lord Dunmore and was forced to move his family to England, where, three years after the close of the Revolution, he died. In his petition loyalist claim to the Lord of the Treasury on August 13, 1778, he said this move was to prevent their suffering from "Every indignity and insult which cou'd be offered to them by a rude and infatuated Rabble." The estate which they had been forced to abandon was most valuable according to the claim. "A dwelling house in the city of Williamsburg the building of which alone cost 4,000 pounds sterling independently of the grounds, gardens, meadows and plantation thereunto belonging." In the midfall of the same year, John Tazewell acquired the property. In the due course of years, Littleton Tazewell, his younger son and later Governor of Virginia, inherited the estate where he lived for a number of years.

The residence is owned by Colonial Williamsburg, Incorporated.

THE ALLEN-BYRD HOUSE

Francis between England and Queen Streets

No. 54 on Williamsburg map

RETURNING to Francis Street by way of England Street, passing the parking entrance to the Craft House, and turning east, one sees the stately Allen-Byrd House. As the Tazewell mansion records the story of a "house divided," so behind the walls of this old home is part of the tragedy of a dissipated fortune. The residence was built just prior to 1770 by William Allen of Surry County, who sold it to William Byrd, the third, of Westover for a city residence. Byrd inherited from his father and grandfather great wealth, but he seems to have spent freely and to have had scant eye for business. Besides Westover, in which his mother had life-interest, he owned a great house in Richmond. On March 14, 1777, the Virginia Gazette published the following advertisement:

"To be Sold Agreeable to the last Will and Testament of the Hon. William Byrd, deceased, at Westover in Charles City County, about 25 miles below Richmond Town, on the 24th of April next, 100 Virginia born slaves . . .

"N. B. The Executrix has also for sale a good Brick Dwelling House with 4 Rooms on each Floor, situated in the city of Williamsburg, lately occupied by the said William Byrd, Esq., and at present by the Reverend John Bracken. The Dwelling house has all convient Outhouses, and several inclosed Lots adjoining; also the very valuable Library of the said Deceased, consisting of near four Thousand Volumes. The House and Library will be disposed of either by private or public Sale as may be most agreeable to the Purchasers."

Thus passed from a famous family a house and a library which, had they been preserved together, would have an interest almost unique. The books were scattered; the residence changed hands often. In the early eighteen hundreds, Judge Samuel Tyler, the district chancellor, lived here. Prior to the War Between the States, John Coke, father of Senator Richard Coke of Texas, owned and occupied the house.

THE BRACKEN HOUSE

Francis and Queen Streets · No. 55 on Williamsburg map

CONTINUING on east Francis Street to the next square on the southeast corner of Queen Street, one is greeted by an old rectory nestled beneath ancient trees. This is the charming eighteenth century home of the Reverend John Bracken, minister of Bruton Parish Church, and even more besides. For one thing, he married Sallie Burwell, a daughter of Carter Burwell, owner of Carter's Grove, James City County, and a great figure among Virginia aristocrats. The Reverend Mr. Bracken himself was a colonial patriot and Professor of Moral Philosophy and President of William and Mary College. At the Episcopal Conventions of the Diocese he served as secretary and later as president. He likewise interested himself in the Eastern State Hospital and headed its court of Directors. In 1812, he was chosen Bishop of Virginia, but resigned his election the following year.

THE ORRELL HOUSE

Francis Street · No. 56 on Williamsburg map

SEPARATED from "the Quarter" by an old and noble weeping willow and the entrance to the Williamsburg Inn is a lovely dutch colonial house, built prior to the Revolutionary War and shown on early maps of Williamsburg. This dwelling, like "the Quarter," has been beautifully restored and furnished for a guest house under the management of the Williamsburg Inn.

THE POWELL-HALLAM HOUSE

Francis Street—Originally on York Street

No. 57 on Williamsburg map

ADJOINING the Orrell house and similar in architecture is the charming gambrel roof house, with an interesting interior, built in 1756, by Benjamin Powell, a wheelwright. The dwelling remained in the Powell family until just before the Revolutionary War. From that time until the spring following the close of the war, it changed ownership countless times before it was conveyed to Augustine Davis, one time editor of the Virginia Gazette. Traditionally this was the home of Miss Sarah Hallam, of the Hallam Company, who settled in Williamsburg as a dancing mistress. She spent her old age here as the cherished pet of the early nineteenth century townspeople who, both old and young, were her frequent callers. One can easily visualize this quaint and famous actress passing under the graceful arch of the entrance hall, pausing to view some treasure in the panelled cupboard or dreaming before the open fire in her gold and green living room.

For many years the residence, on its original location on York Street, was unoccupied and was fast falling to ruin. In 1929, Colonial Williamsburg, Incorporated, moved and rebuilt the dwelling on the present site.

THE MOODY HOUSE

Francis Street · *No. 58 on Williamsburg map*

NEXT DOOR to the Powell-Hallam House, surrounded by beautiful trees is a quaint old story and a half frame dwelling, which speaks for itself as a typical residence of early America. As early as 1800 the property was owned by the Moody family. Fifty odd years later Johnson Sands transferred his interest to Robert Roper, a man of many trades, in whose possession it remained until his death in 1893. In his will he devised the property to his daughter, Mrs. C. D. Lee who owned it until 1928. Today restored and furnished it is used for a guest house under the management of the Williamsburg Inn.

THE CHISWELL-BUCKTROUT HOUSE

Francis Street : No. 59 on Williamsburg map

PASSING the Ewing House, which faces Botetourt Street, and continuing to the middle of the square opposite the Galt House, one arrives at an ancient dwelling whose modern additions conceal its original architecture. Tragedy and reckless adventure are associated with this site. Here, tradition has it, in an earlier house dwelt a sea-faring man who subsequently proved to be Captain Teach, better known as "Blackbeard," the pirate. In 1718 he was killed by Captain Henry Maynard in a hand-to-hand fight off the coast of North Carolina. The surviving members of his gang were brought to Williamsburg, imprisoned in the old Public Gaol on East Nicholson Street, duly tried and convicted and, as noted in the paragraph on the Gaol, ceremoniously hanged on the road to Capitol Landing.

The present dwelling on the supposed site of Teach's house was built in 1750 for Elizabeth Randolph, the bride of Colonel John Chiswell. He was a member of the House of Burgesses from Hanover County, she the daughter of William Randolph of Turkey Island, Henrico County, ancestor of many renowned Americans. Colonel Chiswell was of pioneering spirit and, in 1757, discovered the New River lead mines, which later provided ammunition for the Continental Army. The discoverer of the mines did not live to see them used for independence. In 1766 he had a quarrel with a Scotchman by the name of Robert Routledge and, in the altercation, killed him. Remorseful or despairing, Colonel Chiswell came home to this house and committed suicide. Eight years later his widow sold the property to Benjamin Bucktrout, who kept a tavern here. Subsequently, the house, remodelled, was the residence of Miss Virginia Wise, granddaughter of Henry Alexander Wise, Governor of Virginia.

This house of mingled memories is the property of Colonial Williamsburg, Incorporated.

THE SEMPLE HOUSE

Francis Street · No. 60 on Williamsburg map

THERE ARE no other places of interest on the south side of Francis Street until one reaches the white picket fence that encloses the stately residence known as the Semple House. This beautiful two-story house with its one-story wings and small-pillared portico is painted white. In the spring, when the lilac and wistaria are in blossom, it is one of the loveliest of the restored Williamsburg homes. There is no authentic data as to when this house was built or by whom. Tradition has made it the home of Peyton Randolph, King's Attorney General for Virginia and president of the first Continental Congress, but a recorded deed shows that he owned and occupied the Randolph-Peachy House on East Nicholson street facing Market Square.

Judge James Semple, an eminent professor of law at the College of William and Mary and the successor to Judge Robert Nelson, owned the dwelling in 1799 and it is from him that it derives its name. Judge Semple was the son of the Reverend James Semple of St. Peter's Parish in New Kent County, and he married Anne Countesse Tyler, eldest sister of President John Tyler. After her death, he married Joanna Black McKenzie, great aunt of his first wife. Later this was the residence of Judge John B. Christian, who married Martha Semple, daughter of Judge Semple by his first wife. Judge Christian deeded the property to George P. Scarburgh in the early eighteen-fifties.

BASSETT HALL

Francis Street · No. 61 on Williamsburg map

BETWEEN the Semple and Waller residences, set back from East Francis Street and graced with a lovely garden, stately Bassett Hall, like Wolsey, has "sounded all the depths and shoals of fame." It was built and first occupied, so far as the records show, during the seventeen-fifties by Colonel Philip Johnson, Burgess for King and Queen County. Unfortunately, he became heavily involved in debts which necessitated the sale of his county estate and the lease of his new Williamsburg home. From the private entertainment of great guests, the house descended to "public entertainment" under Richard Hunt Singleton.

On the death of Colonel Johnson, in 1789, Burwell Bassett of the magnificent and now vanished "Eltham," New Kent County, purchased the estate. It was from this nephew of Martha Washintgon that the house received its present name, "Bassett Hall." Bassett lived here for fifty-odd years and received many notables. The Irish poet, Thomas Moore, is said to have written his poem, "To The Firefly," after a summer evening on the portico. Apparently no native marred his delight by telling him that in Virginia the insects which stirred his fancy are styled uneuphoniously, lightning bugs.

At the end of Bassett's days, this property was bought by the astute Abel P. Upshur, a native of Northampton County. He was a great friend of President John Tyler and a member of his cabinet. In the winter of 1844, while on board the Princeton in the Potomac River with Tyler and other members of the Cabinet, Upshur and several others were killed by a gun explosion. This tragedy inspired one of President Tyler's noblest speeches, "The Dead of the Cabinet."

The line of the Williamsburg Restoration passes through the lawn of Bassett Hall, but the fine old residence has been returned to its eighteenth-century splendor and has been refurnished most appropriately.

THE BENJAMIN WALLER HOUSE

Francis and Waller Streets · No. 62 on Williamsburg map

ON THE east side of Bassett Hall estate is the charming Waller residence, which gives one the feeling that it is a part of the knoll on which it stands. In front of this old yellow clapboard dwelling with its steep gable roof and dormer windows is an ancient gnarled apple tree. Leading to its inviting porch, flanked by boxwood, is a flagstone walk bordered by jonquils.

Tradition says this house was built in 1710. Some forty years later it was the home of Judge Benjamin Waller, a prominent citizen and patriot. He was on the vestry of Bruton Parish Church and, by reason of the amplitude of his family and retinue, is said to have procured permission to build a gallery in the church for their exclusive use. Unlike some of the great men who had winter homes in Williamsburg, Judge Waller resided here all the year, shared in the founding of the State Insane Asylum, served as a member of the City Committee on imports, and sat for James City County in the House of Burgesses. At his death his son, Benjamin Carter Waller, inherited the dwelling, which passed in turn to his son, William. Before the end of the first decade of the twentieth century, it became the residence of William H. E. Morecock, one time clerk of James City County in whose family it has remained.

THE ROBERT NICOLSON HOUSE

York Road · No. 63 on Williamsburg map

PASSING the Benjamin Waller house and continuing to the middle of the square, on the left is the attractive story and a half dwelling with shingle roof and half circle steps, built after the middle of the eighteenth century for Robert Nicolson, a tailor, who doubled as the proprietor of a public house. In his home many visitors found shelter during the sessions of the General Court. Otherwise this home, which is privately owned and occupied, is not known to have figured conspicuously in the history of the town.

THE ROBERTSON-GALT HOUSE

Francis Street · No. 64 on Williamsburg map

RETURNING to Francis Street, one stops opposite the Semple House, to visit the Ayscough Shop, so named in honor of Christopher Ayscough and his wife Ann, gardener and cook at the Palace during Governor Fauquier's administration and owners of the property. Here one may watch the cabinetmaker at work in ancient fashion. Crossing the street and driving east, one passes the Robertson-Galt House. Like many of its contemporaries, the dwelling is a story and a half high, with slanting roof and three dormer windows, and is one of the oldest houses in Williamsburg. Tradition makes it originally the home of Major Otto Thorpe, one of the first settlers at "Middle Plantation" and a relative of George Thorpe, who was massacred in 1622. It was here, as legends run, that Nathaniel Bacon, the rebel, held his meeting before the rebellion. Authentic ownership, established by court records of the early seventeen hundreds, begins with William Robertson. As often was the case, the deed to him had a clause which provided that he should build one or more good dwelling houses on the lots, according to the act of the Assembly of 1705, or the lots would escheat. He resided here until 1723, when he sold the house of John Grymes of Middlesex. Grymes was a member of the Council and father of Alice, who married Mann Page of Rosewell. There is a brief gap in the history of the dwelling until the middle of the century, when it was the property of William and Thomas Nelson, and probably was used as the town residence of Thomas. From the Nelsons the property passed at the close of the eighteenth century to the Galt family, representatives of which still own and occupy it. The interior is beautifully panelled and has a "physick closet," a relic of at least two doctors of a family of noted surgeons, Doctors John Minson and Alexander D. Galt.

MERCER HOUSE

Francis and Botetourt Streets · No. 65 on Williamsburg map

LEAVING the Robertson-Galt house and continuing west to the corner of Botetourt Street, one passes several modern bungalows and a small cottage, known as the Wig-Maker's House, before reaching the last of the gracious and typical Williamsburg residences. The date of the erection of this story and a half clapboard dwelling, is unknown. The earliest mention of it is in 1767, when William and James Anderson, blacksmiths, owned it. Later Doctor Philip Barraud, merchant and apothecary, purchased the property. Here he resided until 1802, when he sold the house to Ann Byrd, widow of Otway Byrd, an ancestor of the present owner of Upper Brandon. Since the early nineteenth century, the list of owners constantly changes, but unchanged is the charming old garden enclosed by a white picket fence. Named for one of its twentieth century occupants it is now the private residence of Dr. and Mrs. Archie G. Ryland.

Regretfully, no doubt, the motorist will turn his car east to York Road and Pocahontas Trail.

POCAHONTAS TRAIL

POCAHONTAS TRAIL

Route 60

One proceeds down Pocahontas Trail (Route 60), which follows the watershed between the James and the York. In the eighteenth and early nineteenth centuries, the great estates faced the rivers, the earliest and surest of travel routes, and for that reason not many of the old homes are visible from the highway. In fact, few of them have survived fire, war or slow decay, that trio of ancestral enemies of Virginia. This does not mean that the country is lacking in historical interest. On the contrary, the armies of two American wars have tramped the old roads, and those of a third conflict have thundered down the railroads to embark for France. Nearly all the great figures of Virginia history have traveled here; almost every acre is bound by tradition to the era of James the first. Besides Yorktown, which is our objective, the lower Peninsula boasts of Hampton, one of the earliest settlements, the fine modern city of Newport News and famous Old Point, where frowns Fort Monroe. In this vicinity is also the Mariners Museum, containing a wealth of material of maritime and nautical interest. Just east of Williamsburg, easily reached from the highway, rise the weathered earthworks of Fort Magruder, where the Confederate rearguard challenged the advancing Unionists, May 4 and 5, 1862, immediately after the retreat from Yorktown. Somewhat east of the point where we turn off to Yorktown, but readily accessible, is the field of Big Bethel, scene on June 10, 1861, of the first clash in Virginia that was dignified with the bloody name of battle.

A little over six and a half miles from the corporate limits of Williamsburg, on the right, one comes to the private road that leads to the great estate of Carter's Grove, one of the historic show places of all Virginia. If one is fortunate, a sign at the gate will announce that the grounds and the lower floor of the house are open for inspection. In the event that the owners are in residence, the grounds will be closed. Perhaps a glimpse of the mansion, in its splendid grove, may be had from the highway.

CARTER'S GROVE

Pocahontas Trail · Route 60, James City County

CARTER'S GROVE was originally a part of an eighty thousand acre estate established in 1619 and known as Martin's Hundred. Carter Burwell, grandson of Robert "King" Carter and son of Elizabeth Carter and Nathaniel Burwell, was the builder of the central part of this beautiful Georgian mansion. The accepted date of the construction is 1751, but the English building-authority who was consulted when the house was restored about 1928 expressed the opinion that it was twenty to thirty years earlier. The original plans were drawn by David Minitree, an English architect who was brought to this country by Carter Burwell for that purpose. Tradition says the great part of the work was done by slaves and that the entire cost was £500, a sum that then had a purchasing power eight or perhaps ten times that of today. The estate had passed from the builder to Colonel Nathaniel Burwell, oldest son of Lucy Grymes and Carter Burwell, when, again to invoke tradition, two young Virginians came, ten years apart, to make their addresses to young lady visitors in the stately residence. George Washington had been caught by the bright eyes of Mary Cary, of Williamsburg, and Thomas Jefferson by the charms of Rebecca Burwell, a niece of the host. Strange as it may seem, both these promising young men were rejected.

After both of these disconsolate young Virginians had joined the Revolution, war descended on Carter's Grove. In 1781 Benedict Arnold was defeated by the Virginia Militia in an attempted landing at Burwell's Ferry. Later, while Colonel Tarleton had his headquarters here, his troops gashed with sabres the beautiful carved balustrades as a memento of their visit.

After these unhappy experiences, Colonel Burwell moved to Clark County where, before 1790, he built "Carter Hall." Carter's Grove remained in the Burwell family for nearly three quarters of a century longer, after which it changed ownership constantly until 1927, when the late Archibald McCrae, Esquire, purchased it. Under his and Mrs. McCrae's supervision, the beautiful old mansion regained the elegance of years of long ago.

YORK COUNTY, VIRGINIA

FROM THE calm beauty of Carter's Grove, one drives slowly through the fruit-tree lane back to Pocahontas Trail, and heads east. After a mile or so, and on the right hand side of the road, one observes an historical marker concerning Martin's Hundreds. Less than a mile farther, one turns left over the railroad tracks on Route 174 to Route 170 and Yorktown. The pilgrim is now in the county of York, one of the eight shires into which Virginia was divided in 1634. The county was first called Charles River in honor of Prince Charles, who later became King Charles, the first, of England, but in 1642 the name was changed to York County after James, the Duke of York, subsequently King James, the second. This narrow strip of land, thirty miles long and five miles wide, bounded on the east by the Chesapeake Bay and on the northeast by the York River, is best known in National history as the scene of the culminating victory of the War for American Independence. In Confederate history, York was a theatre of indecisive early operations.

At the foot of the hill just before entering the old town, take the road to the right, up another incline past modern dwellings and stop at the parking space beyond the Swan Tavern.

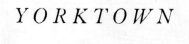

YORKTOWN

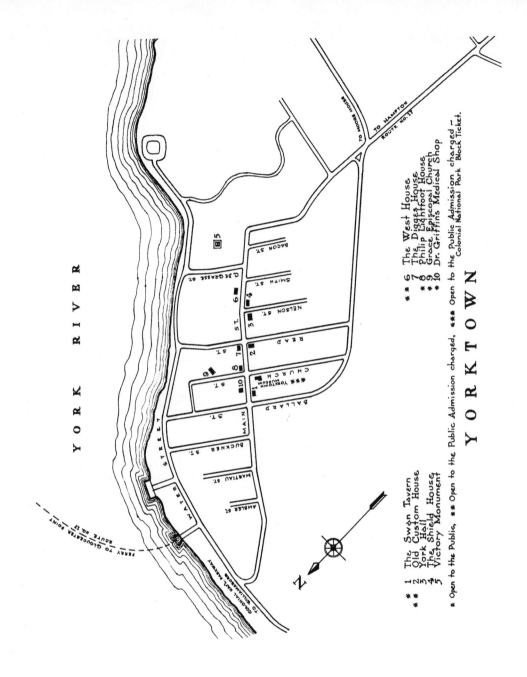

YORK RIVER

YORKTOWN

* * 1 The Swan Tavern
* * 2 Old Custom House
* * 3 York Hall
* 4 The Shield House
5 Victory Monument

* * 6 The West House
* 7 The Digges House
* 8 Philip Lightfoot House
* * 9 Grace Episcopal Church
* * 10 Dr. Griffin's Medical Shop

* Open to the Public, ** Open to the Public Admission charged, *** Open to the Public Admission charged ~
Colonial National Park Block Ticket.

YORKTOWN, YORK COUNTY

BEYOND the reddish rock marl cliffs overlooking the blue waters of the York River and Chesapeake Bay is picturesque Yorktown, founded pursuant to "an Act for Ports" et cetera, passed April 16, 1691, by the General Assembly. The land was obtained from Benjamin Reade, grandson of Nicholas Martiau, first burgess for York County in the General Assembly. The same year, Lawrence Smith surveyed the town which seven years later became the county seat. Save for a lively foreign trade and a pleasant social life, Yorktown was inconspicuous until battle flags and war drums came in 1781. Lord Cornwallis hurried hither in the autumn of that year to establish contact with the British fleet. The French and Americans followed and on October 19, 1781 forced his Lordship to surrender with his entire force.

During the first eleven months of the War Between the States, the Army of the Peninsula, under the command of Major-General John B. Magruder, lay at Yorktown and across the York River at Gloucester Point. His aim was two-fold, "to defend the country between the York and James Rivers against a Federal advance by land from Fort Monroe, and, secondly, to prevent Federal ships from passing up York River to West Point, where they could land troops within less than forty miles of Richmond." In April, 1862, General Joseph E. Johnston assumed command of the operations on the Peninsula, which resulted in the evacuation of Yorktown and in a fierce battle just below Williamsburg. The little town then became the base of supplies for the Federal forces under General George B. McClellan. After the armies passed, peace and quiet came again, to be disturbed no more until the World War when Yorktown became a naval base for the United States Government.

Today Yorktown with its few streets of scattered, ancient houses has been re-created as part of the Colonial National Historical Park. This historical reservation was authorized by an Act of Congress in 1930, and defined by the Presidential Proclamation to include Jamestown Island, parts of the city of Williamsburg, the Yorktown battlefield, including Gloucester Point, and a parkway connecting the three areas. The whole is under the National Park Service, a bureau of the Department of the Interior, which seeks to preserve and develop for the benefit and enjoyment of the people the historical sites and structures within the assigned boundaries. In this area, the visitor may trace colonial history in Virginia, its birth at Jamestown in 1607, its development at Williamsburg, and on to its close at Yorktown in 1781.

To obtain a general idea of the surroundings and to absorb some of the atmosphere of by-gone years, it will be best first to inspect the Park Museum. Here, as in the museum at Williamsburg, one may trace the past through fragments, photographs and maps. The Naval Museum, in the rear, contains a full-size reproduction of part of the gun deck and cabin of a British frigate of the Revolutionary period. This has been furnished throughout with articles salvaged from British vessels sunk off Yorktown in 1781.

THE SWAN TAVERN

Main between Ballard and Church Streets · No. 1 on Yorktown map

THE SWAN TAVERN, Yorktown's most famous Colonial Inn, was built between the years of 1719 and 1722 by Thomas Nelson, Senior, and Joseph Walker. The old story and a half clapboard tavern, with its slanting roof and dormer windows, shared the same fate as its neighbor, the Court House across the street, which was burned during the War Between the States. It was rebuilt only to be destroyed by fire a second time. In 1934 the little building was reconstructed on the original foundations, and the first floor was furnished as a tavern. It is now used by the National Park Service for technical offices of the park.

OLD CUSTOM HOUSE

Main and Read Streets · No. 2 on Yorktown map

TWO FULL BLOCKS farther on, after stopping to peep into at least one or more antique shops, the visitor is in front of the Old Custom House which was built in 1706 and is the oldest structure of its kind in the United States. This staunch and weather-worn brick building looks today as it did over two centuries ago. It still guards American treasures, because it is the home of the Comte De Grasse Chapter of the Daughters of the American Revolution.

The inscription on its wall reads:

EARLY COLONIAL CUSTOM HOUSE

BUILT 1706

YORKTOWN

Was Made A Port Of Entry At A
General Assembly Of The Colony And Dominion
Of Virginia, Begun At The Capitol In The City
Of Williamsburg The Twenty-Third Day Of October
1705 In The Fourth Year Of The Reign Of Her
MAJESTY QUEEN ANNE

THE COMTE DE GRASSE CHAPTER
The National Society Of The
DAUGHTERS OF THE AMERICAN REVOLUTION INC.
Purchased This Custom House 1924

BOARD OF MANAGEMENT
At The Time Of Purchase
MRS. EMMA LEAKE CHENOWETH, Regent
Mrs. Elizabeth Fox Madison
Mrs. Nannie Cooke Curtis
Mrs. Lula Wade Renforth
Mrs. Nettie Richardson Clements
Mrs. Lillie Hudgins Walthall
Mrs. Margaret Crooks Smith
Restored By
MRS. LETITIA PATE EVANS
Member Of The Comte De Grasse Chapter
1929   1930

*Dedicated to Perpetuate
The Memory And Spirit Of The Men And Women
Who Achieved American Independence*

YORK HALL

Main and Nelson Streets · No. 3 on Yorktown map

ACROSS READ STREET behind an ivy-covered brick wall is the beautiful formal garden of the stately Nelson Mansion. The cornerstone of this spacious two and a half story brick residence was laid in 1711 by the infant son of William Nelson, the President of the Council and father of General Thomas Nelson of Revolutionary War fame.

During the siege of Yorktown in 1781 when Lord Cornwallis occupied the house as his headquarters, General Nelson, who was then Governor of Virginia, a Signer of the Declaration of Independence and the owner of Nelson House, ordered the American soldiers to fire upon it. His command was obeyed. The Marks of cannon balls in the eastern wall still are visible.

As a result of the war, the Nelson fortune was greatly impaired by debts contracted for the country's liberty. To meet these demands, everything except this house was sold. It remained the property of the family until the early part of the twentieth century when Joseph Bryan, Esquire, of Richmond, Virginia, purchased it, but it was not until 1920 when Commander and Mrs. George Preston Blow bought York Hall that it was restored to the beauty and charm of former days. Since Mrs. Blow's death, the residence is open to the public as an historic shrine, except from October until spring, during which time it is occupied by the family.

THE SHEILD HOUSE

Main and Nelson Streets · No. 4 on Yorktown map

ONE IS TEMPTED to wander along the narrow lane called Nelson Street which is the eastern boundary of York Hall Estate and peer over the vine-covered wall that encloses its spacious lawn and fascinating quarters, but the time is short, and the lure of the oldest house in Yorktown is great. This little ivy-covered story and a half, brick dwelling, with clipped gables and huge outside chimneys, is made more charming by the contrast of its elegant neighbor.

Built in 1699 by Thomas Sessions, and now known as the Sheild House, it has withstood the ravage of time and wars undamaged. During the War Between the States, the little dwelling was used by General Naglee as his headquarters.

VICTORY MONUMENT

Overlooking York River

Between Comte de Grasse Street and Newport News and

Hampton Roads · No. 5 on Yorktown map

IN VIEW of the Sheild House and two blocks east is the Yorktown Monument, erected by the United States Government in honor of the victory of the American and the French forces. On the one hundredth anniversary of the capture of the town, the cornerstone was laid by President Chester A. Arthur. At that time the monument was known as the Centennial Monument. It was completed in 1884, but not until after the Colonial National Historical Park at Yorktown was established, was it styled officially the Victory Monument, and transferred from the War Department to the Department of Interior. The monument bears the following inscription:

"At Yorktown on October 19, 1781, after a siege of nineteen days by 5,500 Americans and 7,000 French troops of the line, 3,500 militia under the command of General Thomas Nelson and thirty-six French ships of war, Earl Cornwallis, commander of the British forces at Yorktown and Gloucester, surrendered his army of 7,250 officers and men, 840 seamen and 240 standards to his Excellency, George Washington, commander-in-chief of the combined forces of America and France, and to his Excellency, the Compte de Rochambeau, commanding the auxiliary troops of his Most Christian Majesty in America, and to his Excellency, the Compte de Grasse, commanding-in-chief of the naval army of France in the Chesapeake.

"The treaty of peace concluded February, 1778, between the United States of America and Louis XVI, King of France, declares the essential end of the present defensive alliance is to maintain effectually the liberty, sovereignty, and independence, absolute and unlimited, of the United States as well in matters of government as of commerce.

"Erected in pursuance of resolution of Congress, adopted October 29, 1781, and one approved June 7, 1880, to commemorate the victory by which the independence of the United States of America was achieved.

"The provisional articles of peace concluded November 30, 1782, and the definitive treaty of peace concluded September 3, 1783, between the United States of America and George III, King of Great Britain and Ireland, declares his Britanic Majesty acknowledged the said United States, viz: New Hampshire, Massachusetts Bay, Rhode Island and Providence Plantations, Connecticut, New York, New Jersey, Pennsylvania, Delaware, Maryland, Virginia, North Carolina, South Carolina, Georgia, to be free, sovereign and independent States" . . .

Directly south of the Victory Monument and just beyond the Inn on the Newport News and Hampton road is the site of Thomas Nelson's House.

THE WEST HOUSE

Main between Nelson and Comte de Grasse Streets

No. 6 on Yorktown map

RETRACING one's way along the main road and crossing Comte de Grasse Street, one pauses before the ancient gnarled mulberries which grace the entrance to an interesting eighteenth century dwelling. This white frame house with gable roof and dormer windows was built in 1706 by Miles and Imanuel Wills on land bought from the trustees of the town.

During the siege of Yorktown and while occupied by British officers, the building was damaged. Forty years later, it was the property of Elizabeth Nelson, daughter of General Nelson and wife of Major John R. West, for whom the house is named.

THE DIGGES HOUSE

Main and Read Streets · No. 7 on Yorktown map

AFTER walking on for two blocks, with only a longing glance towards York Hall, one is in front of a small and rambling whitewashed brick house. Ivy climbs to the eaves, the thick walls are on the edge of the narrow sidewalk. This is the so-called Digges House, which was built in 1705, by John Martin who eight years later sold it to Cole Digges, sometime member of the House of Burgesses for York County and a member of the council.

Through more than two centuries the staunch old dwelling withstood war, fire and decay. Today, calm and dignified, it is the private residence of Mrs. Carroll Paul who, in 1925, attractively restored it.

PHILIP LIGHTFOOT HOUSE

Colonial National Historical Park Headquarters

Main and Church Streets · No. 8 on Yorktown map

ON THE WEST corner of the same square with the Digges House is a substantial red brick, story and a half dwelling, with an interesting exposed chimney. This house was erected about the year 1710 and six years thereafter was acquired by Philip Lightfoot, surveyor-general of the colony, in whose family it remained for sixty-odd years. Prior to the War Between the States, the old building was still a private residence occupied by Judge Peyton Southall, but after the close of the conflict, a frame addition was made to the rear. For years subsequently the house was known as "Ye Olde Yorktown Hotel." Today the original structure, properly restored, is used for the headquarters of the Colonial National Historical Park.

GRACE EPISCOPAL CHURCH

Church Street, Rear of the Philip Lightfoot House

No. 9 on Yorktown map

AT THE CORNER of Main and Church Streets, the visitor turns right and follows the roadway which leads toward the river until he sees, nestling beneath age-old trees and enclosed by a high wall, an ancient marl edifice with cupola and bell. This is Grace Episcopal Church, originally York-Hampton Church, built in 1697, which from its earliest beginning has been connected with war and disaster. While used as a powder magazine by the British during the siege of Yorktown, it was greatly damaged but not destroyed. Sixty odd years later fire descended upon the small building and almost consumed it. In time it was partially rebuilt and during the War Between the States was used as a hospital for the wounded of the Peninsula Campaign. Today, amid the peaceful and ever interesting graveyard, old Grace Church, in its restored beauty, continues to serve the spiritual needs of the town.

The inscription on the tablet at the entrance to the church is as follows:

COLONIAL GRACE CHURCH
York-Hampton Parish
"A National Shrine at the Cradle of the Republic'
Erected 1697—Burned 1814—Partially Rebuilt 1825—Rebuilt 1926

These are the original walls, built of marl.
The bell was cast in London in 1725.

Broken during fire of 1814. Recast in Philadelphia 1882

The Original Hammered Communion Silver,
Made in London 1649, is still in use.

First Confirmation Service in Virginia
was held in this Church in 1791.

General Thomas Nelson, Jr.
Signer of the Declaration of Independence
Lies buried in the Churchyard.

1936

DOCTOR GRIFFIN'S MEDICAL SHOP

Main between Ballard and Church Streets · No. 10 on Yorktown map

RETRACING one's steps back to Main Street, one reaches what, in days of yore, was Court House Green, where today slightly changed stands the Yorktown Post Office, the reconstructed Medical Shop of Doctor Corbin Griffin. This little one story, white frame building with steep roof, tiny lean-to and huge chimney is believed to be on its original foundation.

Dr. Griffin, one of Yorktown's most distinguished physicians, was born in Lancaster County, Virginia, the son of Mary Bertram and Leroy Griffin. He received his early education at William and Mary College in Williamsburg, and in 1765 graduated from Edinburgh, Scotland. Returning to America, he took an early and active part in the Revolution, and served on the York Committee of Safety and as a surgeon in the State Navy. After the war, Doctor Griffin, who married Mary, the daughter of Colonel Edmund Berkeley of Middlesex County, Virginia, held several important political offices until his death in 1814.

Next to Doctor Griffin's Medical Shop are the nineteenth century Court House and Clerk's Office built on the foundations of their seventeenth century predecessors which were greatly damaged during the War Between the States. In the Clerk's Office one may see ancient and interesting court records that date continuously from 1633.

Returning to the Park Museum, one may secure information or a guide for the battlefield tours and the Moore House. This is a lovely as well as an educational side trip which travels through silent woods, by small modern farms and over good roads. On departure from Yorktown, by way of Ballard Street, one sees on the left-hand side the bronze tablet which marks the site of Nicholas Martiau's House. At the fork of the road beyond the wharf, turn right toward Williamsburg by way of the beautiful Colonial National Parkway, along the sloping banks of the York River and through long winding stretches of woodland.

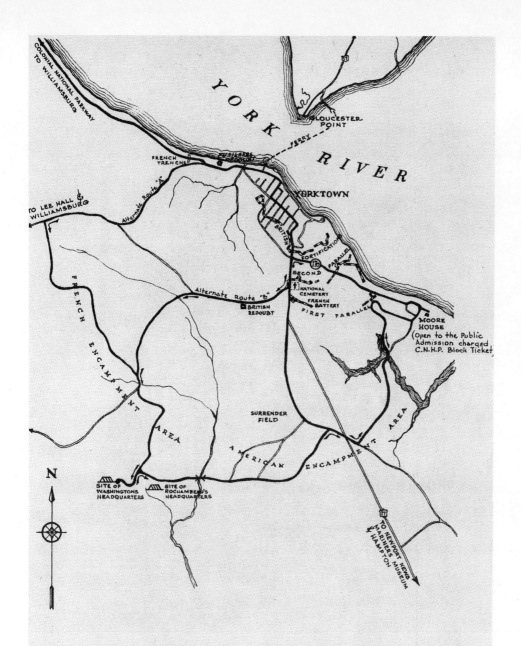

YORKTOWN BATTLEFIELD

MOORE HOUSE

Overlooking York River, Battlefield Tour

THIS TOUR has been designed so the visitor may obtain the complete story of the Siege of 1781 by driving over the same roads used by the Revolutionary soldiers. These roads extend through the battlefield and pass close by the troop encampment positions, headquarters sites, artillery parks, and the restored fortifications.

After the Siege of 1781, the trenches, redoubts and batteries of the French and American armies were leveled, but the National Park Service has restored a large part of these fortifications. The earthworks which now form a semi-circle around Yorktown were thrown up by the Confederates in 1861-62 on approximately the same line as occupied by the British fortifications in 1781.

Surrender Road and Field are to the right of Highway No. 17 on the old York-Hampton Road; the intersection of the roads is reached just after passing the National cemetery going south where over two thousand Union soldiers who lost their lives near Yorktown during the Peninsula Campaign of 1862 are buried.

Cornwallis' troops marched down this road and stacked their arms in the field to the right on the afternoon of October 19, 1781.

Following the arrows and recrossing Highway No. 17, one takes the road to the Moore House. The nearby land was patented about 1631 by Sir John Harvey, Governor of Virginia. A little more than a decade later the lovely dutch Colonial clapboard house with its interesting interior was the residence of Colonel George Ludlow, a member of the council. Here, according to tradition, Colonel Ludlow, with his neighbor, Colonel Ralph Wormeley, from across Wormeley's Creek, entertained Cavalier refugees from England. Following the Ludlow occupancy, "Temple Farm," as it was then called, went to Major Lawrence Smith, whose heirs sold it in 1769 to Augustine Moore. Within its walls, on October 19, 1781, the officers representing Cornwallis and Washington met and drew up the "Articles of Capitulation," which gained America her independence. The dwelling, which has been restored, is open to the public by the National Park Service and is within the boundary of the Colonial National Historical Park. The National Society of the Daughters of the American Revolution have undertaken the refurnishing of the Surrender Room.

Taking leave of the historic building, one walks through the garden and past the ancient kitchen, to the entrance. From this point, one keeps on Route 170 through Yorktown, down Ballard Street, and on back to Williamsburg by way of the Colonial National Parkway.

ROLFE HIGHWAY

ROLFE HIGHWAY

Route 31 · James City County

WITH AN admiring farewell to charming old Williamsburg, one takes the Rolfe Highway (Route 31) for six and a half miles through beautiful wooded stretches, by peaceful lakes and tangled swamps to even more historic Jamestown Island. There, in impressive silence only the ivy-covered ruins of old Jamestown Church, whose weather-beaten walls are almost concealed by memorial tablets, remain to tell the thrilling and glorious story of hunger and starvation, of strife and bloodshed between the White Man and the Red Skin, and the final victory of the English over the Indian. Surrounding the ancient edifice and enclosed by a tall iron fence are time-worn tombstones whose faint inscriptions bring back the past.

JAMESTOWN

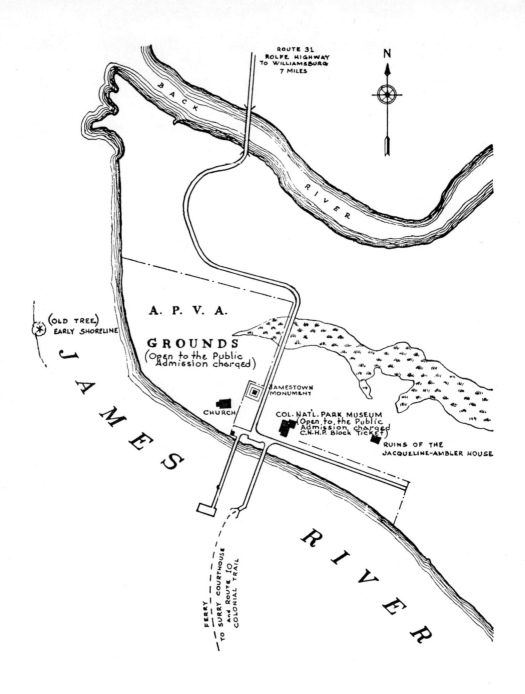

JAMESTOWN

JAMESTOWN

Jamestown Island

FIVE DAYS before Christmas, 1606, the good ships, SARAH CONSTANT, GOODSPEED and DISCOVERY, under the ownership of the London Company, set sail from Blackwall, London. Aboard the squadron were a group of gentlemen, carpenters and laborers, who were to plant a colony on the new continent for the purpose of increasing the wealth, greatness and security of their Mother Country. On May 13, 1607, after many long weeks of rough sea, the little band of voyagers dropped anchor off this sandy beach and established the first permanent English settlement in America, which they called Jamestown in honor of their Majesty, King James, the first.

The island, in reality then a peninsula, was approximately two and a half miles in length and varied in width from five hundred yards to one and a half miles. Marsh lands penetrated the virgin forests which was surrounded on three sides by the James River and separated from the mainland on the north by the Back River. This was the red man's hunting ground. Naturally he resented the white man's invasion and watched him with hostility. Sounds of the axe and the cracking of giant felled trees preceded the hasty construction of a triangular palisade, which was to serve the entire colony as a fort and a town.

On the day after the landing, under the shelter of tall trees before an improvised altar, the Reverend Robert Hunt held the first divine service on Virginia soil. After prayers and thanksgiving, Captain Christopher Newport, who was in command of the expedition, assembled together the men who were to represent the government in the new colony. Before leaving England, he had been given sealed instructions with the names of those who were to comprise the first Colonial Council: Bartholomew Gosnold, John Smith, Edward Wingfield, Christopher Newport, John Ratcliffe, John Martin and George Kendall. Edward Maria Wingfield was chosen the first President of the Colony, but as he had made himself obnoxious, he was deposed, and Captain John Ratcliffe was put in his place.

All was not peace and beauty under calm skies. Wind-swept were the frozen waters during the bitter winters of 1609 and 1610, known in history as the "starving times." Through those long months, the struggling colonists underwent tragic hardships until the late spring of the following year, when Sir Thomas Dale arrived with relief supplies and became High Marshall and acting Governor of the Colony. Two years later, under Dale's governorship, Pocahontas was baptised Rebecca in the second Jamestown Church by Parson Richard Buck, who in the early spring amid dogwood and red bud blossoms, performed the marriage ceremony between this Indian Princess and the Englishman, John Rolfe. Through this union, peace for a time came to the colony, but three years later, while with her husband and son on a visit to England, Pocahontas died. She was buried in the Chancel of St. George's Church, Gravesend, England.

The first General Assembly of Virginia met on July 30, 1619, in the "Quire of the Church" (the third and last wooden one). During the ensuing month two important and far reaching events occurred. The first was the adoption of plans for establishing the earliest college in North America, a few miles below Henricopolis in Charles City County, now Prince George County, to be known as Henrico University and College, which three years after its erection was obliterated by a devastating Indian massacre. The second and far more tragic event was the landing of a Dutch man of war at Jamestown with the first cargo of Negroes whose descendants, less than two and a half centuries thereafter, were one of the causes of bitter long years of strife between the North and the South.

During 1621, George Sandys, the first Anglo-American poet, came to Virginia. The good ship Warwick landed with "an extraordinary choice lot of thirty-eight maids for wives." These fair ones were to marry husbands of their choice, who in return paid for their passage from overseas.

In the spring of 1635, when Sir John Harvey was Governor and Captain-General, the initial but not the final rebellion against tyranny and oppression raged in Virginia. Years rolled on, accumulating discontent of the unprotected people, until 1676, when Nathaniel Bacon, "a gentleman of no obscure family" and the chosen leader of the defenseless planters, led his bedraggled army against Sir William Berkeley, the Governor. With the approach of fall, the hand of fate touched Bacon, who died in Gloucester County from fever and exposure. By midwinter, the entire colony was in submission, but much of the town was destroyed. Subsequent years witnessed a constant struggle between the House of Burgesses and Governor Francis Howard, the bewigged Lord Effingham, due mainly to his oppressive measures. It was not until the accession of King William and Queen Mary to the throne of England in May, 1689, that discontent was finally quieted. Under their regime and the popular administration of Sir Francis Nicholson, the charter for erecting and building the College of William and Mary was granted, the cornerstone was laid at "Middle Plantation" on August 8, 1693, and the College was named in honor of the new royal sovereigns, through whom higher education came to Virginia.

While the new town grew and progressed, the earlier settlement declined and decayed. Five years later, when a disastrous fire entirely destroyed the State House and adjoining prison at Jamestown, the Governor and Burgesses resolved to rebuild them near the contemplated Capitol at "Middle Plantation." Jamestown was deserted for Middle Plantation, which in time became Williamsburg.

Almost one hundred years later, Lord Cornwallis and his forces camped at Jamestown where they had a brush with Lafayette. Here, too, the French troops landed on their way to the siege of Yorktown. There followed years of quiet at Jamestown until the early part of the nineteenth century when the Champion Travis residence, one of the two remaining houses in Jamestown, was completely consumed by fire. Before the War Between the States, the Jacqueline Ambler mansion shared the same fate. Early in the war a Confederate Fort was erected on the island, but was never used.

The Commonwealth of Virginia, in 1892, conveyed to the Association for the Preservation of Virginia Antiquities, which was chartered three years previously, all of its rights in Jamestown. The following year, Mr. and Mrs. E. E. Barney gave the Association twenty-two and a half acres of land surrounding the church yard. Included was the Confederate Fort. All of Jamestown Island, with the exception of these twenty-two and a half acres, was purchased in 1934 by the United States Government and is now a part of the Colonial National Historical Park. In the temporary Museum one may see many fragments found in excavations.

OLD JAMESTOWN CHURCH

Jamestown Island

THROUGH THE iron gates at the river's edge, one enters a sacred precinct and follows the narrow path to the ruins of the first brick church on the island. If one is fortunate and there is no crowd, a feeling of sacred calm pervades the hallowed spot where five churches have stood. The dates of the various Jamestown churches are:

First:	very crude	1607
Second:	wood	1608
Third:	wood	1617–1619
Fourth:	brick	1639–1647
Fifth:	brick (rebuilt)	1676–1686

The original old tower is all that remains of the first brick church, which was burned during Bacon's rebellion. When peace came, it was rebuilt but shortly thereafter was abandoned and gradually was reduced to ruins. The thick high walls which were restored in 1907 by the National Society of Colonial Dames, were copied from St. Luke's Church, the oldest brick Protestant church in America, near Smithfield, in Isle of Wight County. The east window of the church is also a copy of the one in the same ancient house of worship. Some foundations of the older, simpler edifices may be seen from the inside of the church where they have been excavated and preserved.

The inscriptions on the tablets which line the interior walls are as follows:

—1—

"In Memory of the Colonial Governors and Presidents of the Council officially residents at Jamestown 1607-1698.

Edward Maria Wingfield	Captain Nathaniel Powell	Edward Digges
John Ratcliffe	Sir Francis Wyatt	Captain Samuel Matthews
Captain John Smith	Captain Francis West	Colonel Francis Moryson
Captain George Percy	Doctor John Pott	Sir Herbert Jeffries
Sir Thomas Gates	Sir John Harvey	Sir Henry Chicheley
Lord De La Warr	Captain John West	Nicholas Spencer
Sir Thomas Dale	Sir William Berkeley	Francis, Lord Howard Baron Effingham
Captain George Yeardley	Richard Kempe	Nathaniel Bacon
Captain Samuel Argall	Richard Bennet	Sir Francis Nicholson
	Sir Edmund Andros	

"Erected by Society of Colonial Dames of America in the State of Virginia."

324

2

"This stone commemorates Princess Pocahontas, or Matoaka, daughter of the mighty American Indian Chief Powhatan. Gentle and humane, she was the friend of the earliest struggling English colonists whom she nobly rescued, protected and helped. On her conversion to Christianity in 1613, she received in Baptism the name of Rebecca and shortly afterwards became the wife of John Rolfe, a settler in Virginia. She visited England with her husband in 1616, was graciously received by Queen Anne, wife of James I. In the twenty-second year of her age she died at Gravesend, England, while preparing to revisit her native country, and was buried there, in St. George's Church on March 21, 1617."

3

"To the Living Memory of His Deceased Friend

CAPTAINE JOHN SMITH

"Sometime Governor of Virginia, and Admiral of New England
Who Departed This Life the 21st day of June, 1641,
'*Accordaumus Vincere est Vivere*'

Here lies one conquer'd who hath conquer'd kings
Subdu'd large territories and done things
Which to the world impossible would seeme
But that the truth is held in more esteeme
Shall I report his former service done
In honour of His God and Christendome;
How that he did divide from pagans three
There heads and lives, types of his chivalry
For which great service in that climate done
Brave Sigismundus (King of Hungarian.)
Did give him as a coat of arms to weare
Those conquer'd heads got by his sword and speare
Or, shall I tell of his adventures since,
Done in Virginia that large continence?
How that he subdu'd kings unto his yoke
And made those heathen flie as wind dothe smoke
And made their land, being of so large a station,
A habitation for our Christian nation
Where God is glorified, there wants supply'd
Which else for necessaries, must have dy'd
But what availes his conquest now he lyes
Interr'd in earth a prey for worms and flies?
O may his soule in sweet elysium sleepe
Until the keeper that all soules dothe keepe
Returne to judgment, and that after thence
With angels he may have his recompence.

"Presented by Washington Branch, Association Preservation Virginia Antiquities. Replica of Tablet St. Sepulchre's Church, London, Eng."

"In memory of Major-General Daniel Gookin
1612   1687

"A planter of Virginia later a pillar of the Colony of Massachusetts Bay. A soldier, a statesman and above all a constant friend and guardian of the native Indians of New England.
"Massachusetts Society of the Colonial Dames of America."

GEORGE SANDYS
(Bronze Tablet written in Latin)

"Erected by the friends of the Classics in America
Under the auspices of the Classical Association of Virginia."

1929

326

"Thomas Savage, gentleman and ensign; the first white settler on the Eastern Shore of Virginia; hostage to Powhatan, 1608; his loyalty and fearlessness endeared him to the great king who treated him as his son, while he rendered invaluable aid to the colony as interpreter; greatly beloved by Debedeavon, the laughing king of Accawmackes; he was given a tract of 9,000 acres of land, known as Savage's Neck. He obtained food for the starving colony at Jamestown through his friendship with the kindly Eastern Shore Indians. A relation of his voyages on the great bay in search of trade for the English was read before the London Company at a court held July 10, 1621. John Pory, secretary of the colony, says; 'He with much honesty and good success served the publique without any publique recompense, yet had an arrow shot through his body in their service'."

Erected by some of his descendants, 1931.

7

"John Rolfe, an English gentleman, came to Virginia in 1610 and in 1622 he was a member of the Council and Secretary of State. In 1614 his marriage with Pocahontas caused a period of good feeling between the Indians and the colonists. As a member of the General Assembly of Virginia in 1619 he was one of the founders of American Democracy. His introduction of the cultivation of tobacco 1612 and his making the first shipment from Virginia to England made him the pioneer of a great industry which has profoundly affected the economic, social and business history of our country. —The Tobacco Association of the United States has erected this Monument as a grateful tribute to his memory.—1926."

"William Claiborne, Secretary of State, and one of the most notable Virginians of the 17th Century."—Given by Mrs. W. R. Cox.

"In grateful memory of Thomas West, Third Baron Delaware, Governor of Virginia, 1609, Saviour of the colony in the starving time of 1610. He died on his second voyage to Virginia 1618.—Given by Mrs. deBenneville Keim."

"In honor of Chanco, the Christian Indian boy whose warning saved the Colony of Virginia from destruction in the massacre of 22 March, 1622. —Erected by the Society of Colonial Dames of America in the State of Virginia."

TO THE GLORY OF GOD
AND IN GRATEFUL REMEMBRANCE OF
THE ADVENTURERS IN ENGLAND
AND
ANCIENT PLANTERS IN VIRGINIA
WHO THROUGH EVIL REPORT
AND LOSS OF FORTUNE
THROUGH SUFFERING AND DEATH
MAINTAINED STOUT HEARTS
AND LAID THE FOUNDATIONS
OF OUR COUNTRY
THIS BUILDING IS ERECTED BY THE
NATIONAL SOCIETY OF COLONIAL DAMES
OF AMERICA
TO COMMEMORATE THE
THREE HUNDREDTH ANNIVERSARY OF
THE LANDING OF THE
FIRST PERMANENT ENGLISH SETTLERS
UPON AMERICAN SOIL
THE 13th OF MAY
1607   1907

THE OLD CHURCHYARD

Jamestown Island

STEPPING OUT into the sunlight and shadows of the old churchyard, one may linger long among the ancient tombstones, some now gone beyond recognition. Here are buried Lady Frances Berkeley, wife of Governor William Berkeley and later wife of Colonel Philip Ludwell; John Ambler, attorney at law, and the Reverend James Blair and his wife, Sarah Harrison, between whom has grown a sycamore tree, the branches of which spread protecting arms and give a peaceful solemnity to the scene.

The wall around the graves is a gift of Mr. Ambler and Mr. Lee of Green Spring; the wrought iron fence enclosing the churchyard was donated by Mrs. Joseph Bryan of Richmond; and the gates were presented by a branch of the Association for the Preservation of Virginia Antiquities.

One could spend hours wandering over this small bit of land where each step brings to the memory some historic episode in the molding of America. Today, memorials tell the tale of heroic events. The inscriptions of these memorials listed in order of approach are as follows:

ASSOCIATION FOR THE PRESERVATION OF VIRGINIA ANTIQUITIES' AREA MARKERS AND MEMORIALS

ENTRANCE GATES

" 'Colere Coloniarum Gloriam'

1607   1907

Wrought iron gates designed by Carrere and Hastings.
Presented by the Society of Colonial Dames of America—
State of New York. May 9, 1907."

BARNEY MEMORIAL

"In lasting gratitude to Mr. and Mrs. Edward E. Barney for the gift of this historic ground, May 3, 1893.
"Placed by A. P. V. A. 1912."

BRONZE STATUE OF POCAHONTAS

"Pocahontas

1595   1617

Modelled

By

William Ordway Partridge

Presented

By

Pocahontas Memorial

Association of Washington, D. C.

1922"

HOUSE OF BURGESSES

"In honor of the first General Assembly of Virginia. Here on the thirtieth day of July, A.D. 1619, summoned by Sir George Yeardley, Governor-General of Virginia, under authority from the London Company, pursuant to the charter granted by King James I, was convened in the church at Jamestown the first General Assembly of Virginia. This Assembly, composed of the Governor, the Council of State and two Burgesses elected by the people from each of the eleven Plantations, was the beginning of Representative Government in the colonies of England and laid the foundation of the liberties of America.

"Also in honor of Sir George Yeardley, Governor-General, Sir Edwin Sandy, Treasurer of the London Company, and Henry, Earl of Southampton, his successor, for their distinguished services in obtaining for the Colony of Virginia the ordinance and Constitution of Government dated November 18, 1618, under authority whereof the first General Assembly of Virginia was held here, July 30, 1619.—Dedicated by the Norfolk Branch of the Association for the Preservation of Virginia Antiquities, July 30, 1907.

" 'Sir George Yeardley, the governour, being sett down in his accustomed place, those of the counsel of estate sat next to him on both handes, excepte only the Secretary, then appointed speaker, who sat right before him. And forasmuche as men's affaires doe little prosper where God's service is neglected, all the Burgesses tooke their places in the quire till a prayer was said by Mr. Bucke, the minister, that it would please God to guid and to santifie all our proceedings to his owne glory and to the good of this Plantation.'

"The Council of Estate: Capt. Francis West, Master John Rolfe, Capt. Nathaniel Powell, Rev'd William Wickham, Master John Pory, Master Samuel Macock.

330

"The Burgesses: For James Citty, Capt. William Powell, Ensign Wm. Spence; For Charles Citty, Samuel Sharpe, Samuel Jordan; For the Citty of Henricus, Thomas Dowse, John Polentine; For Kiccowtan, Capt. Wm. Tucker, William Capp; For Martin Brandon (Captain John Martins Plantation) Mr. Thomas Davis, Mr. Robert Stacey; For Smythes Hundred, Capt. Thomas Graves, Mr. Walter Shelley; For Martin's Hundred, Mr. John Boys, John Jackson; For Argall's Guifte, Mr. Pawlett, Mr. Courgainy; For Flowerdieu Hundred, Ensigne Rossingham, Mr. Jefferson; For Capt. Lawne's Plantation, Capt. Christopher Lawne, Ensign Washer; For Captaine Ward's Plantation, Capt. Ward, Lt. Gibbes."

GENERAL CONVENTION OF THE EPISCOPAL CHURCH

"In Memory of October 15, 1898, when the pious pilgrimage to this Island was made by 300 Bishops and Clergy of the Protestant Episcopal Church accompanied by many like minded patriots.

"They shall perish but thou shalt endure. Thou art the same. Thy years shall have no end.

"Ps. 102-26-27.—Erected by A. P. V. A."

CAPTAIN JOHN SMITH MONUMENT

"Vincere Est Vivere"

Captain John Smith

Governer

of

Virginia

1608

By William Couper

Presented By

Mr. and Mrs. Joseph Bryan

of Richmond, Virginia

Unveiled

May 13, 1909

(Erected by A. P. V. A. 1907 on Mt.)

331

CONFEDERATE FORT

"Confederate Fort erected by order of General Robert E. Lee—1861."

ENGLISH ANCESTORS

"A tribute to the Heroism of our English Ancestors at Jamestown, Virginia, 1607, presented by the Society of Daughters of Colonial Wars Massachusetts.—1928."

THE REVEREND ROBERT HUNT MEMORIAL

"Commemorating the celebration of the first Holy Communion in the New World. By Gorham Co. and presented by the Episcopal Dioceses of Virginia, Southern Virginia and West Virginia.—1907.—Dedicated June 15, 1922.

1607-1907

"To the glory of God and in memory of the Reverend Robert Hunt, Presbyter-Appointed by the Church of England minister of the colony which established the English Church and English civilization at Jamestown, Virginia, in 1607. His people, members of the colony, left this testimony concerning him: 'He was an honest, religious and courageous Divine, he preferred the service of God in so good a voyage to every thought of ease at home, he endured every privation, yet none ever heard him repine.' During his life our factions were oft healed and our greatest extremities so comforted that they seemed easy in comparison with what we endured after his memorable death. We all received from him the Holy Communion together as a pledge of reconciliation for we all loved him for his exceeding goodness. He planted the first Protestant Church in America, and laid down his life in the foundation of Virginia."

Geo. T. Brewster Sc.

BRONZE DRINKING FOUNTAIN

"A gift of the General Society of Colonial Wars."

YEARDLEY HOUSE

"This house is said to be a Colonial reproduction from the design of 'Malvern Hill,' in Henrico County. It was erected in 1907. The Daughters of the American Revolution presented it to the Association for the Preservation of Virginia Antiquities. It is used as a residence for the manager and caretaker of this historic shrine."

332

FOUNDATIONS OF STATE HOUSE, LUDWELL HOUSE
AND THE COUNTRY HOUSE (PUBLIC STORE HOUSE).

"These foundations were discovered and identified in 1903, by Samuel Yonge, Designer of the Sea Wall and author of 'The Site of Olde Jamestown 1607-1698.'

"Placed by A. P. V. A. 1907

"Built about 1666. Burned during Bacon's Rebellion in 1676. Rebuilt and burned in 1698. The excavation and preservation were due to Mr. Samuel H. Yonge.—1903."

THE RELIC HOUSE

This small modern building, erected by the United States Government, houses many interesting relics of the Island which various excavations have brought to light. It is also a rest room for visitors.

SEA WALL

Erected by the United States Government, 1901-1903, to prevent further encroachment of the river upon Jamestown Island.

JAMESTOWN MONUMENT

Jamestown Island

LEAVING THE Association for the Preservation of Virginia Antiquities area, one visits the Jamestown Tercentenary Monument before boarding the ferry to continue one's journey home along the southern banks of the James. Inscription on the monument reads as follows:

"Jamestown, the first permanent Colony of the English People, The Birthplace of Virginia and of the United States May 13, 1607.

"Lastly and chiefly the way to prosper and achieve good success is to make yourselves all of one mind for the good of your country and your own, and to serve and fear God the giver of all goodness, for every plantation which our Heavenly Father hath not planted shall be rooted out.

"Advice of London Council for Virginia to the Colony 1606.

"Representative Government in America Began in the First House of Burgesses assembled here July 30, 1619.

"Virginia Company of London, Chartered April 10, 1606, Founded Jamestown and Sustained Virginia 1607-1624.

"This Monument Was Erected by the United States A. D. 1907 to Commemorate the Three Hundredth Anniversary of the Settlement Here."

SURRY COUNTY, VIRGINIA

AFTER A pleasant quarter of an hour or so on the ferry crossing the lower James River, one lands at Scotland on the south side, in Surry County, which was formed from James City County in 1652 and was named for the Shire of Surrey, England. It is a compact area, about twenty miles on each axis. James River skirts its northern border; along part of its southern boundary flows the Blackwater River. Due to its strategic position, Surry County was the scene of several engagements during the Revolution and the War Between the States.

SMITH'S FORT PLANTATION

Rolfe Highway · Route 31, Surry County

AFTER LEAVING the Scotland ferry and driving two and a half miles on Rolfe Highway to Surry County Court House, there is, on the right hand side of the road, a charming little story and a half, red brick house with three dormer windows at equal intervals in its gabled roof. This small dwelling, with two rooms on each floor, panelled mantels and carved cupboards, was built in 1652 by Thomas Warren, a member of the first House of Burgesses for Surry County. Tradition affirms it to be the oldest brick residence in Virginia, though this is disputed. Thomas Rolfe, son of Pocahontas and John Rolfe and grandson of Powhatan, the Indian Chief, once owned this property. As so often is the case, after countless changes of ownership, the land and buildings degraded into a sad state of dilapidation. In 1933, the property was purchased and presented to the Association for the Preservation of Virginia Antiquities by John D. Rockefeller, Jr. The Association has authentically restored the quaint abode to its former charm and beauty. Under the supervision of the Garden Club of Virginia, the grounds surrounding it have been tastefully and appropriately planted. The ancient dwelling and the pathways through the woods to the meager remains of "Smith's Fort" are open to the public.

SURRY COUNTY COURT HOUSE AND OLD CLERK'S OFFICE

"The Cross Roads," Surry County

ONE DRIVES a fraction over a mile and a half on Rolfe Highway before reaching the quiet little village at "the Cross Roads." When the county seat was moved here from Troopers in 1797, the Court House was erected on land given by Robert McIntosh, an innkeeper who was also the contractor for the building. After a hundred years, less two, the first court house was razed to make way for a larger one which unfortunately was shortly destroyed by fire, as was its handsomer successor. The present Court House was completed in 1923 and contains county records dating back to 1652.

In the courtyard still stands the original old clerk's office, built in 1825-26, which housed these ancient records until the erection of the 1896 Court House. From then until 1905 the tiny brick house was the headquarters for the Surry Cavalry organization. Today it is a museum and Chapter House of the Surry County United Daughters of the Confederacy.

COLONIAL TRAIL

COLONIAL TRAIL

Route 10

LIKE Old Indian Trail in Henrico and Charles City Counties, Colonial Trail in Surry, Isle of Wight and Prince George Counties runs by well cultivated farms and through shady stretches of woodland to many lovely old estates, quaint dwellings and ancient churches. We shall visit, in order of their approach, only a few of these famous places. To reach Colonial Trail from Scotland, follow Rolfe Highway to Surry County Court House and turn east at "the Cross Roads." If interested in old churches, after leaving Bacon's Castle, turn left on Colonial Trail and continue east through Smithfield to "Old Brick Church in Isle of Wight." To see this age-old shrine necessitates a détour of approximately thirty miles because it is necessary to retrace the route to Surry County Court House, where Colonial Trail leads west through Prince George County to City Point.

There are various old buildings of historic and architectural interest which, because of inaccessibility or years of neglect, remain secluded. We shall not disturb their solitude but merely mention a few. Near Claremont was Wakefield, the original home of the Harrison family, but unfortunately now only the site remains. Not far from Cabin Point is Montpelier, another home of the distinguished Harrison family, which at present is not available for tourists as the road is very poor. Other old homes on lower Colonial Trail in Surry County are Rich Neck, once the stately ancestral home of the Ruffin family, Mount Pleasant, one time residence of the Cocke family, and Pleasant Point, which was patented in 1657 by William Edwards, Clerk of the Council, and remained in the possession of his heirs until 1812. Last but not least is Four Mile Tree, an ancient brick story and half dwelling with two chimneys at each end of its gambreled roof. The terraces and high boxhedges bring visions of past beauty, while in the orchard-graveyard is the oldest legible inscription on a tombstone in Virginia. The plantation received its name from a tree on this property which, in 1619, marked the western limit of the Corporation of Jamestown.

CHIPPOKES

Colonial Trail · Route 10, Surry County

TAKING COLONIAL TRAIL, one drives east for four and a half miles before reaching, on the left, the private entrance to Chippokes, an ancient sixteen hundred acre plantation on the south side of the lower James River.

One half of this land was first granted to Captain William Powell, who came to Virginia in 1611. He was a member of the First House of Burgesses and was killed in the massacre of 1622. His son, George, inherited it and in 1642 leased three hundred acres to Stephen Webb, who promised to build thereon "one good and sufficient framed house underpinned with brickes." Within the year George Powell died. As there was no direct heir, the property reverted to the Crown.

Sir William Berkeley, who came to Virginia as Governor in 1641, received a grant for the other half of the plantation and two years later acquired the part previously owned by Powell. Since that date the boundaries have not changed. From Sir William, the estate passed to his widow, Lady Berkeley, who married Colonel Philip Ludwell, the first. Thus coming into the possession of the Ludwell family, it was left by will of the third Colonel Philip Ludwell to his daughter Lucy, who married John Paradise of London and became the Madam Paradise of Williamsburg fame. During the Ludwell ownership, the old clapboard dwelling house, with gable roof and dormer windows, was enlarged to the present size on the original location, where it commands a magnificent panoramic view of the lower James.

In 1838, Albert Carroll Jones acquired the property, but it was not until 1856 that he completed the present brick residence, which for the past twenty-odd years has been the home of Mr. and Mrs. Victor W. Stewart. Chippokes of the twentieth century radiates the charming atmosphere of years of long ago, but the highlight of this estate is the five-mile plantation drive over fertile fields, through shadowy woods down to the sandy beach at the river's edge.

BACON'S CASTLE

Colonial Trail · Route 10, Surry County

ONE TURNS LEFT on Colonial Trail and pauses in passing to see the picturesque vine-covered ruins of Lawnes Creek Parish Church, which was built in the middle seventeen hundreds and burned during reconstruction days. Across the road through distant trees one sees the chimneys of Bacon's Castle. Turn left at the Historical Marker and one is within a half mile of the beautiful old grove that surrounds this staunch and time worn building.

Tradition says the house was built in 1655 by Arthur Allen of England, who had come to Virginia about ten years previously. At his death, his son, Major Arthur Allen, sometime Speaker of the House of Burgesses, inherited the property, which remained in the Allen family until well into the nineteenth century. This unusual old brick residence of Jacobean architecture is two full stories high with a livable attic. At each end of its interesting, gabled roof is a huge brick chimney which tapers gracefully into three smaller ones. Through the long years, many and varied additions have greatly changed the original appearance of the structure and have deprived it of the architectural characteristics of any particular period.

During Bacon's Rebellion, the home was seized and used as a fort by the Rebel's adherents and since then has been known as "Bacon's Castle." Today, after a long line of conveyances, the old house is the residence of Mr. and Mrs. Walker Pegram Warren.

ISLE OF WIGHT COUNTY, VIRGINIA

ISLE OF WIGHT COUNTY is one of the original eight shires and was first called Warrosquyoake after an Indian tribe, but, in 1637, was changed to Isle of Wight County after the island in the English Channel.

One hundred and ten years later, the little town of Smithfield in the northern part of the county, about three miles from the James River on Pagan Creek, was laid out. Here, for the past hundred years and more, the inhabitants have exported their celebrated hams and bacon. The only historical place of interest in the county which is included in our pilgrimage is St. Luke's Episcopal Church, more often spoken of as "Old Brick Church in Isle of Wight."

ST. LUKE'S EPISCOPAL CHURCH

Colonial Trail · Route 10, Isle of Wight County

FOUR MILES EAST of Smithfield one enters, by way
of new and impressive gates, the road leading up the hillside to a grove
of age-old trees and to St. Luke's Church. This ancient and beautiful
Gothic edifice, not unlike the vine covered ruins of Old Jamestown
Church, was built in 1632 under the supervision of Joseph Bridger and
is the oldest brick Protestant Church in America. "Old Brick Church,"
as it is traditionally called, was originally in Warrosquyoake parish,
which was divided several times between 1642 and 1752, when it became Newport Parish.

During the Revolutionary War, the inhabitants in
the vicinity, hearing of the intended raid by the British troops under
Tarleton, hurriedly buried the county records and the vestry books in
an old trunk, but unfortunately when peace came and they were dug
up, many crumbled to pieces.

In 1830 the church ceased to be used and remained
in neglect and growing dilapidation for the next sixty years until it
was restored to its former beauty and usefulness.

THE GLEBE

Colonial Trail · Route 10, Surry County

RELUCTANTLY LEAVING the quiet beauty surrounding Old Brick Church, one retraces the journey back to Surry County Court House. Here, at "the Cross Roads," turn left, continue on Colonial Trail west for a little over four and a half miles and slow down, in passing, to view from the highway the old Glebe. The location, of this old Dutch colonial red brick house, corresponds to the two hundred acres of land granted to Martin's Brandon Parish for a glebe during Governor Berkeley's administration in 1667. The dwelling is said to have been erected in 1742 as a residence, possibly for the Reverend John Cargill, minister of Southwark Parish at that time.

The present-day Glebe, with its pillared porches and modern additions, enclosed by a white picket fence, is a dairy farm.

EASTOVER

Colonial Trail · *Route 10, Surry County*

FOUR MILES WEST of the old Glebe is Spring Grove. Here one turns right to the Patrick Henry Highway (Route 40) to Eastover. Just before reaching the entrance to Eastover estate, one passes on the left a small sign marked "Fludd's." This ancient plantation house was once an attractive residence but is now a dilapidated hovel, the name of which has even changed. In 1638, when Surry County was still a part of James City County, John Flood, Indian interpreter for the Colony, patented some two thousand acres of land on the south side of James River. Nearly twenty years later, Colonel Henry Browne, a prominent early settler in this section, conveyed to George Jordan "a parcell of land . . . lying in Surry County upon James River" adjoining "ye westermost end of pipsco plantation." This land was probably a part of the original grant to Captain Henry Browne in 1637.

Four years after America gained her independence, Robert Watkins acquired the plantation from Charles Harrison, son of Benjamin Harrison, of Berkeley in Charles City County. Early in the eighteen-forties, the estate was willed to John A. Selden, Jr., one time owner of Westover, the adjoining land to Berkeley. Unfortunately, Eastover shared the fate of many other Virginia homes during the War Between the States when Federal gunboats used it for a target.

Through the long years of various ownership, the boundaries and acreage vary, but even today Eastover contains twenty-five hundred acres of land which includes the original land deeded by Colonel Henry Browne to George Jordan in 1657 and the plantation patented by John Flood. The present two-story, clapboard dwelling with its more recent one-story wings is directly opposite the Chickahominy River. It is situated on a high cliff which commands a sweeping view of the James. As at Chippokes, the land slopes gracefully to lovely wooded ravines. Between the residence, which is owned by Mr. and Mrs. Albert Henry Ochner, and the much older story and a half quarter house is a charming boxwood garden. Flanking the land front of the small dwelling, is a row of gnarled mulberry trees.

CLAREMONT MANOR

Colonial Trail · Route 10, Surry County

AT THE Eastover and Claremont Ferry sign, one makes a sharp right turn and drives a fraction over five miles to the entrance to Claremont Manor, where, in 1649, over twelve thousand acres of land were granted to Arthur Allen, the builder of Bacon's Castle. Unlike Bacon's Castle, this residence is said to be a copy of Claremont Manor in Surrey, England, which was once the home of the Duke of Kent, Queen Victoria's father. Shaded by giant trees and surrounded by dwarf-box and stately magnolias, this Virginia counterpart of the English seat is one of the most beautiful estates on the lower James. It is a brick house, T in shape and one and a half stories high with clipped gables and dormer windows. The entrance from the road faces the many old and inviting plantation houses, among which are the four story office, the loom house, a bake house and two smoke houses. This view of the house is most unusual, with the main entrance in the center of the bottom of the T. A high wall on either side reaches to the eaves of the roof and forms a porch and court on each side. On the river side, the lawn slopes through an avenue of lindens to the river where one gets a distant view of Jamestown Island and the Brandons.

The plantation remained in the Allen family for over two centuries. During the first four generations it descended in direct line, after which it was inherited by a cousin, Colonel William Allen, a member of the convention of 1788, who was followed by his son, William Allen, Junior, a colonel in the War of 1812. At his death the property was willed to his great-nephew, William Orgain, provided he take the name of Allen. This he did, serving as Major William Allen in the War Between the States. After the death of the Major in 1875, the estate was divided and sold.

In 1928 the late Brigadier-General William Horner Cocke and Mrs. Cocke bought the lovely old mansion from Mr. and Mrs. Meredith A. Johnston. Under their guidance the residence was remodelled and the gardens and the grounds were beautifully restored.

Since 1940 the elegant old seventeenth century estate has been the residence of Mr. and Mrs. Ronald Balcom.

GRACE EPISCOPAL CHURCH

Cabin Point on Colonial Trail · Route 10, Surry County

LEAVING Claremont Manor gates, turn right when reaching the Y fork and head towards Colonial Trail and Cabin Point where, on the left, almost concealed by clinging vines and high weeds, is the lovely but abandoned Grace Episcopal Church. The mellowed stucco of its sturdy walls and stately towers, with gracefully arched but glassless windows, add a weird charm to its loneliness and neglect. The date of the building of this old Southwark Parish church is unknown.

PRINCE GEORGE COUNTY, VIRGINIA

TAKING LEAVE of the weird charm of the old Southwark Parish Church in Surry County, one drives west a few miles
and is in Prince George County which, until 1702, was that part of
Charles City County located on the south side of the James River.
At that date, all land in Charles City County on the south side of the
river was established as Prince George County and was christened in
honor of Prince George of Denmark, the husband of Queen Anne.
This county, like most of the others mentioned, is bounded by navigable rivers, the James on the northeast and the Appomattox on
the northwest. Among the flourishing commercial centers are Petersburg, Hopewell and City Point. They, too, have played their part in
the making of history through the long years of peace and war.

BRANDON

Colonial Trail · Route 10, Prince George County

FOLLOWING a byroad to the right at Burrowsville, one drives more than ten miles through shadowy woods, by fertile fields, to Brandon before returning by way of Upper Brandon to the highway. This enormous tract of land was patented in 1616 by Captain John Martin, a member of the first Virginia Council, and known as "Martin's Brandon." Twenty odd years later, Captain Robert Bargrave, thought to be the grandson of Captain John Martin, sold the property to Symon Sturgis, John Sadler and Richard Quiney, of London. Subsequently, Richard Quiney left his share to his son, Thomas. He in turn willed it to Robert Richardson, his great nephew, who in 1720 sold the estate to Nathaniel Harrison of Wakefield, Surry County. There are many and varying dates for the erection of the present house, but there is no authentic record. In 1735, Nathaniel Harrison, the second, made additions to the dwelling, possibly one of the two story wings, in themselves small but comfortable houses which at one time faced each other. It is thought, however, after Thomas Jefferson's return from France, that the central portion of the residence was built from plans drawn by him and that at a still later period the one story passages connecting the main part with the wings were constructed.

This spacious and stately mansion of many beautifully proportioned rooms is situated in a majestic grove of ancient trees. Strolling over the velvety lawn hedged by shaggy bush box, one reaches the broad grass path, edged by low growing shrubs and shaded by towering elms and age old yews, which ends on the cliff overlooking the river. At intervals, narrow walkways entice one to the various little gardens, each outlined by dwarf box enclosing old-fashion flowers.

In the spring of the first year of the Revolutionary War, the British forces under General Phillips landed here. Less fortunate during the War Between the States, Brandon was a target for Federal gunboats, ransacked and damaged. Years rolled on, while the plantation remained in the Harrison family, under whose regime its far flung fame was established, until 1926, when the late Gordon Harrison sold it to the present owner, Robert Williams Daniel.

UPPER BRANDON

Colonial Trail · Route 10, Prince George County

PASSING BACK through the entrance gates of Brandon, one turns sharp to the right on the farm road, opposite Brandon stables, which leads to Upper Brandon, once a part of Martin's or lower Brandon. The large and lovely house, surrounded by giant willow oaks, was built in the early eighteen hundreds by William Byrd Harrison, youngest son of Benjamin Harrison of Brandon and grandson of William Byrd, the third, of Westover. At the death of William Byrd Harrison, the estate passed to George Harrison Byrd, his nephew and the father of the present owner, Francis Otway Byrd.

During the War Between the States, the residence was occupied by Federal soldiers who, as usual, left their sabre gashes on the balustrades and bullet holes in the panelled walls. One of the four sons of the owner, who were defending the South, namely, Captain Benjamin Harrison, was killed in the Battle of Malvern Hill. During those years the beautiful old garden suffered much and has never recovered its full glory, although there still are traces of the terraced boxwood and the serpentine pathways at the end of a box-bordered walk which leads from the front of the mansion to the river's edge. Upper Brandon, which is not so elegant, but a bit more massive than its elder neighbor, has retained a charm and atmosphere found only in the homes which have remained in the same family from generation to generation.

BRANDON EPISCOPAL CHURCH

Colonial Trail · Route 10, Prince George County

THE DRIVE from Upper Brandon back to Colonial Trail follows a road parallel to the one to Brandon and joins it just before reaching Brandon Church at the fork of the road on the highway. The first written records of Martin's Brandon Parish are in 1712, when the Reverend John Worden was minister to Weyanoke and Martin's Brandon Parishes. These parishes were divided eight years later; that on the north side of the James River was, as now, known as Westover Parish and those on the south side of the river as Martin's Brandon and Southwark Parishes.

The little building, like most of the old Virginia churches, suffered greatly during the wars and was for many years unused. The present church, which serves the surrounding community, was built near the site of "Old" Brandon Church.

APPOMATTOX MANOR

Pecan and Brown Avenues, City Point

THE THIRTEEN-AND-A-HALF-MILE drive from old Brandon Church to Appomattox Manor is over a straight, rather monotonous highway, broken now and then by peanut fields, tidy farms and woodland. Upon reaching the Hopewell railroad tracks, turn right and follow closely the mileage chart of streets until you arrive at the settlement of City Point, which was established in the winter of 1613 by Sir Thomas Dale and called Bermuda City, later Charles City Point. Across from City Point, at the mouth of the Appomattox River, in 1621 was the East India School, which, in the early spring of the following year, during the fatal Indian Massacre, was entirely destroyed.

Thirteen years after the massacre, Colonel Francis Epps, later to become a member of his Majesty's Council, patented this large tract of land on which, in the middle of the seventeen hundreds, he built the present house, for which he used materials of its predecessor nearer the river. During the War of Independence, General Phillips and his forces landed here on their way to Petersburg, enroute, the troops set fire to the dwelling, which fortunately was saved by faithful slaves.

At intervals during 1862-63, the residence was fired upon by northern gunboats, but during the siege of Petersburg it was General Grant's headquarters and a Federal hospital. It was here that President Lincoln visited General Grant when Richmond was evacuated.

This historic frame residence, with its dormer windows and many porches, is still owned and occupied by a direct descendant of Colonel Francis Epps.

371

CHESTERFIELD COUNTY, VIRGINIA

LEAVING APPOMATTOX MANOR, past the business section of Hopewell and striking the United States Highway No. 1, one is in Chesterfield County and well on the way back to Richmond and the Capitol Square. Chesterfield County until 1748 was that part of Henrico County situated on the south side of the James River. Skirting its northern line is the James River and on its southern boundary flows the Appomattox. Among the many places of interest within its confine are historic Bellona Arsenal, established in 1816, adjacent is Bellona foundry, one of the oldest cannon foundries in the United States, the Midlothian coal mines, in operation since 1833, and Salisbury, one of the many residences of Patrick Henry. Unfortunately, our pilgrimage is practically at an end and does not lead in their direction.

When reaching Manchester, since 1911 known as South Richmond, one is immediately opposite Richmond. Here one crosses James River, by way of Mayo's Bridge, the last of a succession of bridges on the same site dating from 1788 when the first span was completed by Colonel John Mayo at his own expense. This was the beginning of a long series of mishaps, from floods, freshets and thawing ice, which necessitated its rebuilding seven times before the twentieth century.

Back in Richmond, turn left on Main Street, drive through the financial district to Ninth Street; then turn right, and one is in full view of the State Capitol.

*If the Pilgrim travels homeward with a deeper
spirit of reverence and appreciation of the past
and, with a renewed courage and inspiration for
the future the journey will not have been in vain.*

E. V. H.

ACKNOWLEDGMENTS

AFTER TEN YEARS of research, compiling of notes and information concerning historical places in Virginia, on the Peninsula and its vicinity, "Peninsula Pilgrimage" emerges from the press. The writer wishes to express her sincere appreciation to Doctor Douglas Southall Freeman, biographer, historian and editor, for his valuable suggestions and gracious introduction which made this work possible.

To the late Doctors Lyon Gardiner Tyler, LL.D., and William Glover Stanard, LL.D., thanks are due for their kindness in checking dates and historical data in the early stages of preparation.

The writer is also indebted to Colonial Williamsburg, Incorporated, for the never failing personal help of its late director of the Department of Research and Record, Mr. Harold R. Shurtleff; its present director, Doctor Hunter D. Farish; its former archivist, Mrs. Helen Bullock, and to Mr. Bela W. Norton, director of Public Relations. To the Colonial National Historical Park through its former superintendent, Doctor B. Floyd Flickinger; its present superintendent, Mr. Elbert Cox; and his assistants, Mr. Edward M. Riley, junior historian, and Miss Olive Drinkwine. To Mr. Morgan P. Robinson, state archivist of Virginia, Miss Helen McCormack, director of the Valentine Museum, the late Miss Susan B. Harrison, house regent of the Confederate Museum, the late Mr. Robert A. Lancaster, Jr., librarian of the Virginia Historical Society, all of Richmond, Virginia; Doctor Earl Gregg Swem, librarian of the College of William and Mary, and the clerks of the various court houses.

To the excellent and untiring help rendered by Mrs. Hawes Coleman, Jr., in the typing and retyping of the manuscript, and to Misses Dorothy Irvine and Madelaine Bigger, who so ably assisted. The writer is also grateful to Mrs. Samuel C. Ramage for her kindness in helping check the bibliography.

Sincere thanks are expressed to the owners, known and unknown, who extended the hospitality of their homes and rendered service in straightening the line between tradition and fact. To the following she is particularly indebted: Mrs. James Harrison Oliver of Shirley, Mrs. John

375

Douthat of Upper Weyanoke, Mrs. Archibald McCrae of Carter's Grove, Mrs. Victor W. Stewart of Chippokes, the Misses Smith and Mrs. Theodore Rogers of Williamsburg and to all other persons who have so generously given their time and encouragement in making this publication possible. Last but not least, the writer is indebted to those who made or loaned the photographs reproduced in this volume, namely the late Mr. Waller Holladay, Mr. A. L. Dementi, the Richmond Chamber of Commerce, Colonial Williamsburg, Incorporated, and the Colonial National Historical Park.

To Mr. Ro. McLean Whittet is due sincere thanks for his untiring efforts in making "Peninsula Pilgrimage" a beautiful book.

E. V. H.

BIBLIOGRAPHY

MANUSCRIPT RECORDS

CALENDAR OF VIRGINIA STATE PAPERS, Vol. I, p. 261,587.

COURT HOUSE RECORDS:
  Charles City County
  Henrico County
  James City County
  Surry County
  York County

EXECUTIVE JOURNALS OF THE COUNCIL, Vol. II, pp. 1, 2 and 339.

GOOCH PAPERS, Vol. III, p. 815.

SAINSBURY ABSTRACTS, Vol. V, pt. 1, p. 74.

WILL OF J. HENRY ISHAM, November 13th, 1678.
  In possession of James Pinckney Harrison.

BOOKS - BOOKLETS

ANDREWS, MATTHEW PAGE, *Virginia The Old Dominion.* Garden City, New York, Doubleday, Doran and Company, 1937.

BOHANNAN, A. W., *Old Surry.* Petersburg, Virginia, Plummer Printing Company, Inc., 1927.

BURTON, LEWIS W., *Historic Henrico Parish and Old St. John's Church,* Richmond, Virginia, 1611-1904. Ed. and Compiled by J. Staunton Moore. Richmond, Virginia, Williams Printing Company, 1904.

CHRISTIAN, W. ASBURY, D.D., *Richmond, Her Past and Present.* Richmond, Virginia, L. H. Jenkins, 1912.

Colonial Churches in the original colony of Virginia. A series of sketches by especially qualified writers. Thirty-five illustrations. 2nd Ed., Rev. and improved. Richmond, Virginia, Southern Churchman Company, 1908.

Encyclopaedia Britannica, 14th Ed., Vol. 15, p. 110.

EZEKIEL, HERBERT T. and GASTON LICHTENSTEIN, *The History of the Jews of Richmond 1769 to 1917.* Richmond, Virginia, Herbert T. Ezekiel Printer and Publisher, 1917.

FRARY, I. T., *Thomas Jefferson, Architect and Builder*. Richmond, Virginia, Garrett and Massie, 1931.

GOODWIN, THE REVEREND EDWARD LEWIS, D.D., *The Colonial Church in Virginia*. Milwaukee, Morehouse Publishing Company and A. R. Mowbray and Company, London.

GOODWIN, RUTHERFOORD, *A Brief History of and Guide Book to Jamestown, Williamsburg and Yorktown*. Richmond, Virginia, Press of Cottrell and Cooke, Inc., 1930.

HENING, WILLIAM WALLER, *Statutes at Large*—Vol. III, p. 55. Vol IV, p. 447— (1711, 1736). Vol. V, pp. 263, 302 (1738, 1748).

HENRY, WILLIAM WIRT, *Patrick Henry's Life, Correspondence and Speeches*. New York, Charles Scribner's Sons, 1891.

History of the College of William and Mary From Its Foundation, The, 1693 to 1870. Baltimore, Maryland, John Murphy and Company, 1870.

HOWE, HENRY, *Historical Collections of Virginia*. Charleston, South Carolina, Babcock and Company, 1845.

KERNODLE, LOUISE NURNEY, *Guide Book of the City of Richmond*. Richmond, Virginia, Central Publishing Company, Inc., 1931.

LANCASTER, ROBERT A., JR., *Historic Virginia Homes and Churches*. Philadelphia and London, J. B. Lippincott Company, 1915.

LEE, EDMUND JENNINGS, M.D., *Lee of Virginia, 1642-1892*. Philadelphia, 1895.

MASSIE, SUSANNE WILLIAMS, *Homes and Gardens in Old Virginia*. Ed. Susanne Williams Massie, Frances Archer Christian. Richmond, Garrett and Massie, Incorporated, 1931.

MEADE, BISHOP, *Old Churches, Ministers and Families of Virginia*. Philadelphia, J. B. Lippincott Company, 1894.

SALE, EDITH TUNIS, *Colonial Interiors*. New York, William Helburn, Inc., 1930.

SALE, EDITH TUNIS, *Ed. Historic Gardens of Virginia*. Compiled by The James River Garden Club. Ed. Edith Tunis Sale. Richmond, Virginia, The William Byrd Press, 1923.

SALE, EDITH TUNIS, *Interiors of Virginia Houses of Colonial Times*. Richmond, Virginia, William Byrd Press, Inc., 1927.

SMITH, MARGARET VOWELL, *The Governors of Virginia*. Washington, W. H. Lowdermilk and Company, 1893.

SMITH, MRS. SYDNEY, *Old Yorktown and Its History*. Historian of Comte de Grasse Chapter, D. A. R. [Richmond Press, Inc., Printers c. 1920.]

STANARD, MARY NEWTON, *Colonial Virginia, Its People and Customs*. Philadelphia and London, J. B. Lippincott, 1917.

STANARD, MARY NEWTON, *Richmond; Its People and Its Story*. Philadelphia and London, J. B. Lippincott Company, 1923.

STANARD, MARY NEWTON, *The Story of Virginia's First Century*. Philadelphia and London, J. B. Lippincott Company, 1928.

STANARD, WILLIAM G., *Notes on a Journey on the James, Together With a Guide to Old Jamestown*. Compiled for the A. P. V. A., 1912.

TYLER, LYON GARDINER, LL.D., *The Cradle of the Republic*. Richmond, Virginia, The Hermitage Press, Inc., 1906.

TYLER, LYON GARDINER, LL.D., *Encyclopaedia of Virginia Biography*. New York, Lewis Historical Publishing Company, 1915. Vol. I, p. 152. Vol. II, p. 54.

TYLER, LYON GARDINER, LL.D., *Williamsburg*, Richmond, Virginia, Whittet and Shepperson, 1907.

Washington His Person as Represented by the Artists. The Houdon Statue its History and Value. Published by the order of the Senate of Virginia. R. F. Walker, Superintendent of Public Printers, 1873. [Senate Document No. XXI.]

WEDDELL, ALEXANDER WILBOURNE, F.R.G.S.; LITT.D. ED., *Virginia Historical Portraiture*. Richmond, Virginia, The William Byrd Press, Incorporated, 1930.

Who's Who in America. 1930-31, p. 918.

YONGE, SAMUEL H., *The Site of Old Jamestown, 1607-1698*. Richmond, Virginia, Published by the A. P. V. A., 1904.

PERIODICALS

TYLER'S QUARTERLY HISTORICAL AND GENEALOGICAL MAGAZINE. Lyon G. Tyler, M.A., LL.D., Editor. Vol. III, No. 4, p. 299. April, 1922. Historical and Genealogical Notes.

VIRGINIA MAGAZINE OF HISTORY AND BIOGRAPHY. Virginia Historical Society. Richmond, Virginia, Old Dominion Press, Incorporated.

Vol. II, No. 3, p. 243. January, 1895. Virginia Officers and Men in the Continental Line.

Vol. III, No. 2, p. 158. October, 1895. Charles City County Grievances 1677.

Vol. V, No. 2, p. 217. October, 1897. Historical Notes and Queries.

Vol. X, No. 1, p. 107. July, 1902. Notes and Queries.

Vol. XI, No. 1, p. 89. July, 1903. Virginia Militia in the Revolution.

Vol. XXXII, No. 1, p. 48. January, 1924. Virginia Councils Journals 1726-1753.

Vol. 605-1418—(from the transcripts in the Public Record Office, London.)

Vol. XXXII, No. 4, pp. 411, 412. October, 1924. The Colonial Royalls of Virginia. John Royall Harris.

Vol. XLI, No. 4, pp. 278, 279. October, 1933. The Society's Home is Being Enlarged and Improved. R. A. L. Jr.

Vol. XLIII, No. 3, pp. 200-208. July, 1935. The Rolfe Property. Anne Page Johns.

VIRGINIA COUNTIES; those resulting from Virginia Legislature. Printed in the Bulletin of the Virginia State Library. Vol. IX, Nos. 1, 2 and 3, January, April, July, 1916.

VIRGINIA COUNTIES; THOSE RESULTING FROM VIRGINIA LEGISLATURE. Printed in the Bulletin of the Virginia State Library. Vol. IX, Nos. 1, 2 and 3, January, April, July, 1916.

WILLIAM AND MARY COLLEGE QUARTERLY HISTORICAL MAGAZINE. Published by William and Mary College.

1st series Vol. II, No. 2, pp. 91-97. October, 1893. *The Lightfoot Family.*

1st series Vol. II, No. 3, pp. 204-207. January, 1894. *The Lightfoot Family.*

1st series Vol. II, No. 4, pp. 259, 262. April, 1894. *The Lightfoot Family.*

1st series Vol. III, No. 2, pp. 104-111, 137. October, 1894. *The Lightfoot Family.*

1st series Vol. III, No. 2, pp. 114-115. October, 1894. *Peachey Family.*

1st series, Vol. III, No. 4, p. 225. April, 1895. *Some Letters of William Beverley.* Contributed by Worthington Chauncey Ford.

1st series Vol. V, No. 1, p. 105. July, 1896. *The County Committees of 1774-75 in Virginia.*

1st series Vol. V, No. 3, pp. 189-191. January, 1897. *Old Places in Surry County.*

1st series Vol. V, No. 3, p. 196. January, 1897. *Descendants of the Rev. Rowland Jones, First Rector of Bruton Parish, Virginia.* Wilson Miles Cary.

1st series Vol. V, No. 3, p. 213. January, 1897. *Historical and Genealogical Notes.*

1st series Vol. XI, No. 1, p. 76. July, 1902. *Historical and Genealogical Notes.*

1st series Vol. XI, No. 4, pp. 260-261, 264. April, 1903. *Munford Wills.*

2nd series Vol. VIII, No. 4, pp. 218, 221-224. October, 1928. *Some Notes on the Four Forms of the Oldest Buildings of William and Mary College.* E. G. Swem.

Index